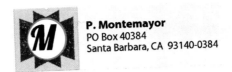

# ALL THE CONSPIRATORS

D1475238

# ALL THE CONSPIRATORS

## CARLOS BULOSAN

*Introduction by*

Caroline S. Hau *&* Benedict Anderson

UNIVERSITY OF WASHINGTON PRESS

SEATTLE AND LONDON

Copyright © 1998 Carlos Bulosan and his heirs
Introduction Copyright © 1998 by Caroline S. Hau and Benedict Anderson
Originally published in 1998 by Anvil Publishing Inc., Philippines
Published by arrangement with Anvil Publishing, Inc.
First University of Washington Press edition published in 2005
Printed in the United States of America

11 10 09 08 07 06 05    5 4 3 2 1

University of Washington Press
P.O. Box 50096
Seattle, WA 98145-5096, U.S.A.
www.washington.edu/uwpress

Library of Congress Cataloging-in-Publication Data

Bulosan, Carlos.
All the conspirators / Carlos Bulosan ; introduction by Caroline S. Hau and Benedict Anderson.
   p.  cm.
Includes bibliographical references.
ISBN 0-295-98497-x   (pbk. : alk. paper)
   1. World War, 1939–1945—Philippines—Fiction.   2. Conspiracies—Fiction.
3. Philippines—Fiction.   I. Title.
PR9550.9.B8A78   2005
813'.52—dc22                                                    2005000292

All materials in the Appendixes are reproduced with the permission of the University of Washington
Libraries, Special Collections, UW23895z (p. 153); UW23896z (p. 154); UW23897z (p. 155); UW23898z
(p. 156); UW23911z (p. 157); UW23908z (p. 158); UW23909z (p. 159); UW23910z (p. 160).

# CONTENTS

# INTRODUCTION

Carlos Bulosan's writings con-
tinue to attract new generations of readers. This might be ascribed
as much to the careful and loving attention with which Bulosan
scholars have endeavored to study him[1] as to the felicitous manner
in which his work retains its relevance to our present concerns
and to the questions we are learning to ask about literature
and society. Bulosan himself, however, gave neither reader nor
scholar an easy time by making provisions for posterity. On the
contrary, he seems to have deliberately set out to defy, but also
court, the whims of time and space. In a letter to Florentino B.
Valeros that we will keep returning to in the course of this
essay, Bulosan wrote: "Now a long time ago I made a resolution never
to reveal certain facets of my personal life; I resolved also not to give to
anyone a complete bibliography of my published writings."[2] Although
the same letter included a partial bibliography that Bulosan compiled
as a favor to Valeros's wife (who was doing her thesis on his writings),
he confessed to giving away, even destroying, hundreds of his own
poems, stories, and articles. At one time, he simply forgot some of them
in a drawer when he moved out of the room he was renting.

The fact that some of Bulosan's writings—including the
novel that you now hold in your hands—survived the deliberate
risks to which he exposed them speaks well of the friends he
made, the University of Washington Libraries, and the efforts of
those whose lives his work has touched to save a writer from his
most implacable enemy, oblivion. As if these circumstances were
not trying enough, Bulosan would confound his audience by giving conflicting information about his life. Biographer Susan
Evangelista writes: "Besides the fact that there is no final, com-

prehensive compilation of his writings, three different dates have been given for his birth, several different opinions of how much schooling he had, and at least two conflicting assessments of the socioeconomic status of his family."³ The account of Bulosan's life that Evangelista has managed to piece together may be summarized as follows:

Carlos Bulosan was born on November 2, 1911, in the village of Mangusmana, Binalonan in Pangasinan. As far as his education is concerned, Bulosan reached high school before leaving the Philippines for the United States. He arrived in Seattle, Washington, in 1931. His poems began appearing in Filipino papers and in an anthology edited by an American woman, Helen Hoyt, who is said to have introduced him to a number of the American literati. Bulosan spent the years from 1936 to 1938 in the Los Angeles General Hospital undergoing treatment for tuberculosis. During this time he read voraciously. He acquired a deep and abiding interest in political and social theory, notably Marxism and socialism. The war years saw more of his poetry appearing in print, including the collections *Letter from America* in 1942 and *The Voice of Bataan* in 1943. His stories appeared in various American serials such as *The New Yorker* and *The Saturday Evening Post*. A collection of Filipinized folk tales from around the world was published under the title *The Laughter of My Father* in 1944. He finished his best known work, *America Is in the Heart*, in 1946. In the early fifties, plagued by ill health and alcoholism, he edited a Yearbook for the International Longshoremen's and Warehousemen's Union (ILWU) Local 37, the predominantly Filipino union of cannery workers in Seattle. Until his death on September 11, 1956, he continued to write poetry, fiction, essays, and even one-act plays, although few if any of these were published in his lifetime.

The critical work done on Carlos Bulosan has cemented his reputation as a committed writer who articulated the realities and collective revolutionary struggles of Filipinos in America and in the Philippines against racism and neocolonialism. He has also been celebrated by ethnic studies programs in America for his pioneering contribution to the shaping of Asian American political and cultural consciousness. In 1960, Dolores Feria edited a collection of Bulosan's letters, *Sound of Falling Light: Letters in*

*Exile*, but critical interest in Bulosan's radical aesthetics, spearheaded by Epifanio San Juan Jr., received the most crucial impetus from the radicalization of Philippine politics during the late sixties. Parallel developments in the States ensured that *America Is in the Heart* would find and in some ways even create a new readership among the generation of Asian Americans whose consciousness of identity was shaped by the civil rights and the anti-Vietnam War movements. San Juan's efforts as an academic working in America have borne fruit with the posthumous publication there and in the Philippines of Bulosan's prose and poetry, including a novel about the Huk movement, *The Cry and the Dedication*, which appeared in the Philippines under the seemingly apposite title *The Power of the People* in 1986. Another longtime U.S. resident, Licerio Lagda, obtained a number of hitherto unpublished manuscripts from Bulosan's friends and associates, including Bulosan's partner, Josephine Patrick, to whom Bulosan had entrusted many of his writings. Some of these were compiled by Lagda and subsequently published as *The Power of Money and Other Stories* by Kalikasan Press in the early 1990s. It is largely through Lagda's efforts of ten years ago that *All the Conspirators* finally appears in print for the first time.

The story of how the novel broke through the surface of the publishing world after decades of subterranean existence reads rather like a mystery novel if only for the intricacy of its plot and the feats of literary deduction that it asks the reader to perform.

The story began when freelance writer Licerio Lagda returned to the Philippines to cover Benigno Aquino's death anniversary in 1984, and enrolled in the Master's program in English at the University of the Philippines.[4] Working on Bulosan, Lagda tracked down and interviewed Bulosan's few surviving friends and associates, including Josephine Patrick, who had been Bulosan's partner during the later years of his life. From these interviewees, and particularly from Patrick, Lagda obtained a number of Bulosan manuscripts, among them a carbon copy of the typescript of *Conspirators*. He then deposited the Bulosan papers in the University of Washington Libraries in Seattle. Lagda prepared some annotations on the unpublished novel, a copy of which he gave to Prof. Elmer Ordoñez of the University of the Philippines. Ten years later, in a separate incident, Prof. Benedict Anderson of

Cornell University visited the University of Washington campus for a lecture, and, while browsing through the Bulosan archives, came across *Conspirators*. He passed on a copy of the manuscript to Karina Bolasco, publishing manager of Anvil Publishing. Following the paper trail of the manuscript led Anderson back to Lagda's notes. You who now hold the novel in your hands therefore represent the final link in the chain. Bulosan himself would have appreciated the fact that the publication of *Conspirators* involved an intellectual conspiracy—in the sense of a joint effort, not all of it concerted, toward a particular end—that extended across two continents over a time span of more than forty years.

But obscurity and rediscovery, it seems, have not exhausted the tribulations of *All the Conspirators*. The process of authenticating the manuscript has often seemed as interminable as getting it published has actually proven to be. The name that appears on the byline of the manuscript is one "Dunstan Peyton," which immediately raises the question of the novel's authenticity. This is not without its precedents, since Licerio Lagda had previously posed the same question in connection with two stories in *The Power of Money* that carried the byline "Josephine Kundle," Patrick's maiden name. On the matter of *Conspirators*, however, Lagda expressed his strong belief that the novel is authentic Bulosan.

The name Dunstan Peyton actually appears in yet another manuscript that can be found in the University of Washington Libraries, a short story entitled "The Filipino Houseboy." On the upper left corner of its first page, the name Dunstan Peyton was typed above a Los Angeles P.O. Box number. In an interview with Licerio Lagda, Josephine Patrick stated that Dunstan Peyton is the pen name that Bulosan used when he submitted the manuscript of *Conspirators* to his literary agent. We might thus presume that Bulosan had also intended to use the pen name Dunstan Peyton for "Houseboy." But what distinguishes the manuscript of "Houseboy" from that of *Conspirators* is the fact that "Dunstan Peyton" also appears *within* the text of "Houseboy" as the main character of the story. Unlike the two stories that appeared in *Money*, both of which have a first-person female American narrator, "The Filipino Houseboy" and *Conspirators* are told from the point of view of a white American male. However, the typescript of "The Filipino Houseboy" contains handwritten corrections which elide the first-person narrator "I" and substitute for it a third-person narrator-character named Dunstan Peyton; the pen name and P.O. Box address on the upper left corner of the first page have also been crossed out.

Interestingly enough, the Filipino houseboy's name, Conrado Bustamante, shows up again in the final chapters of Bulosan's Huk novel, *The Cry and the Dedication*, this time as the real name of protagonist Dante, one of the members of the Huk mission to Manila.

Lagda has stated that he finds the prose style of *Conspirators* consistent with that of Bulosan's other writings. But perhaps the strongest and, at the same time, the most problematic evidence in favor of the authenticity of the manuscript is provided by Bulosan himself. In two separate letters—the aforementioned one to Florentino B. Valeros in 1955, and an undated one to Josephine Patrick—Bulosan mentions *All the Conspirators* by name. In the letter to Valeros, Bulosan describes it as one of "five [projected] novels centering around the Filipino theme on the Pacific Coast."[5] The other four novels are *The Hound of Darkness* ("Hound" is pluralized on page three of the letter: "I have a novel, *The Hounds of Darkness*, it is like nothing of its kind."), *A Door Against the Setting Sun*, *What Fools We Are*, and *The House Almanzor*.

We mention these novels because they, too, play a starring role in a related mystery, this one involving yet another novel, *The Cry and the Dedication*. In his introduction to the American edition of *Cry*, San Juan writes that the earlier draft of *Cry* went by the title *Hounds of Darkness*, citing as evidence the above passages from Bulosan's letter to Valeros.[6] The trouble with this claim, though, is that in that same letter, Bulosan attached a fourth page, a partial bibliography containing a reference to "FIRST DRAFTS OF-THE CRY AND THE DEDICATION, an 800-page novel based on the Huks movement" (the manuscript of *Cry* in the University of Washington Libraries, by the way, has 442 pages). If, as San Juan states, the first draft of *Cry* went by the name of *The Hounds of Darkness*, one wonders why Bulosan would refer to *Cry* and *Hounds* by different names in the same letter.

One possible explanation suggests itself when we read the letter more carefully. Bulosan ends his letter with a note explaining that "the letter attached has been written off and on for several days because of the scramble in this office [i.e., the office of the ILWU where he worked]." If Bulosan worked on sections of the letter as well as the partial bibliography over a couple of days, could he have decided to use *The Cry and the Dedication* in the partial bibliography as the (final) title of *Hounds of Darkness?* It could very well have happened that he decided to jettison *Hounds*, settled on *Cry* as the new title, subsequently used the new title in his bibliography without correcting the old title that he mentioned twice in the body of the letter, and finally mailed the letter and its attached bibliography to Valeros, blissfully unmindful of the headache that he would cause subsequent generations of scholars.

Although San Juan attributes *Hounds of Darkness* to *The Cry and the Dedication*, it is equally possible that *Hounds* could be the working title of *All the Conspirators*. After all, *Hounds* would probably have made more sense as a working title for *Conspirators* than for *Cry*, given that being in pursuit and being pursued appear to be the main activities of protagonists and antagonists alike in *Conspirators*. One can comfortably imagine both the savory and unsavory characters in *Conspirators* as "hounds of darkness" since death invariably follows in their wake. But this is all speculation. Perhaps, true to its title, *Hounds of Darkness* has yet to see the light of day.

But there is more to the question of authentication than the present confusion surrounding *Hounds of Darkness*, and this leads us back to *Conspirators*. As if establishing Dunstan Peyton as one of Bulosan's pseudonyms (he admitted to using the name Cecilio Baroga in that same letter to Valeros) were not problem enough, the second mention that Bulosan makes of *Conspirators*, this time in a undated letter to Josephine Patrick, includes a plot summary that in no way resembles the plot of the manuscript entitled *All the Conspirators* that Lagda obtained from Patrick.[7] The plot summary of *Conspirators* (and, incidentally, of *The Hound of Darkness*) provided by this undated letter is consistent with Bulosan's assertion in his letter to Valeros concerning the five projected novels "centering around the Filipino theme on the Pacific Coast." Now, two different explanations can be advanced to account for these discrepancies. Either Bulosan did not write the *Conspirators* novel under discussion, or, as Lagda speculates, Bulosan may have changed his mind after telling Patrick about the original plot of *Conspirators* and made it a thriller/mystery novel instead.[8]

We are inclined to agree with Lagda's judgment on the strength of the evidence of the handwritten corrections, the prose style of the novel with its quaint idioms and non-native speaker's phraseology, and, as we will argue in the following section of this essay, the content of the novel. We shall try to argue thus by reading *Conspirators* against *Cry and the Dedication*.

Let us begin by noting that there may be another reason why some readers will be cautious about accepting *Conspirators* as a Bulosan oeuvre. Critical perspectives on Bulosan have based their claims about Bulosan's radicalness as a writer on the strength of Bulosan's ability to effect the marriage between politics and aesthetics. In the letter to Valeros (again!), Bulosan explicitly stated that his "politico-economic ideas are embodied in all [his] writings, but more concrete[ly] in poetry." A cursory reading of *Conspirators* is bound to disappoint students of Bulosan who expect the kind of committed writing that they have encountered in *America Is in the Heart* and *The Cry and the Dedication*. These last two have generated readings that have conferred upon Bulosan's work the rightful status of "serious" and "revolutionary" literature. But here in *Conspirators*, we encounter a different Bulosan, not the Bulosan who wrote the unfinished verses about Rizal, but the Bulosan who adapted his short story about the Amorous Ghost into a one-act play.

*All the Conspirators* follows Gar Stanley, a white American, as he returns at the end of World War II to the land of his childhood, the Philippines, in order to help an old flame, Candy, locate Clem, her missing husband, who happens to be Stanley's best friend. Clem was a guerilla leader who, along with his daughter from a previous marriage, Tampa, disappeared following an ambush by Japanese troops. The plot centers around the mysterious reappearance of the missing man's ring. Stanley's attempt to track down his best friend takes him from the war-ravaged city of Manila to the seemingly idyllic mountains of Baguio, from bordellos to churches, from nightclubs to Igorot huts. He meets people representing a cross-section of society—bankers, bored society matrons, mistresses, nightclub singers, mestizos ("halfbreeds"), thugs, Igorot chieftains, street urchins, and hoboes.

Throughout the search, two men keep materializing at the most crucial moments—Pepe Gonzales, the suave, nonchalant mestizo scion of a landed family; and Goyo, a slovenly, hard-drinking man of the streets. It is Goyo who provides the key explanation regarding the ring: "During the war, I saw that ring. Whenever it appeared in Manila, it meant a message of some kind. I do not know what the message was. The ring was passed among us to the other until it reached a certain man. He knew what it meant. But we were always happy when we saw the ring. We knew that it came from a group of guerillas and that they were planning something."

Who the ring is meant for certainly remains a mystery until almost the end. The reader automatically assumes that Gar Stanley is the recipient of the "message," but Stanley's efforts to locate the owner of the ring bring him face to face with a variety of people, from the obvious minatory thugs and the corrupt banker who offers to buy his complicity to not-quite-so innocent victims who pay for the information they divulge with their lives. Along the way, Stanley finds his sympathies gradually being drawn toward the downtrodden and the highlanders. The trust that he initially places in certain people turns out to be misplaced (displaced, too). For, as the title of the novel implies, in the postwar Philippines, separating the collaborators from the noncollaborators is not easy. In fact, it turns out to be a much harder task than Stanley can manage as the hero of the novel. In the end, the person he most distrusts, Pepe, comes to his rescue and reveals himself to be a government agent assigned to collect evidence against the collaborators. Conversely, his trust in his former girlfriend Candy makes him an unwitting dupe of the collaborators, who use him to track down and kill his best friend.

The protagonist/narrator of the novel is an American who, despite the fact that he grew up in the Philippines and can speak one of the native languages, is bound to annoy some Filipino readers with his macho remarks about the Philippines and about women (sometimes he appears to conflate the two), and his cynicism about oiling the wheels of daily existence in the Philippines with money. For those who have more than a skimming acquaintance with *America Is in the Heart* and *The Cry and the Dedication*, this short novel reads like an unassuming potboiler, replete with an inordinate amount of coincidences, happenstance, and Gar Stanley's corny asides. How did Bulosan go from writing the paradigmatic Filipino American *Bildungsroman* and, better yet, classic Filipino *litterature engagée* to a "commercial" novel about an American tracking down a missing fellow-American in the Philippines?

But perhaps we ought to begin not by evaluating the novel in light of Bulosan's other novels, but by examining the connections between them. Again, we note that the name "Dunstan Peyton," which appears in the byline of the title page as the author of *Conspirators*, shows up as the narrator/character in the short story "The Filipino Houseboy." In "The Filipino Houseboy," Peyton is described as an American novelist who is pleasantly surprised by the hardworking, courteous, and efficient ministrations of his Filipino houseboy, Conrado Bustamante. There are clear parallels between Bulosan and Bustamante, from the shared initials of their names to the fact that Bustamante, like the Bulosan of *America Is in the Heart*, worked as a houseboy for an American at a young age and went on to write bestselling books. We would suggest, however, that there are also links between Dunstan Peyton and the real Carlos Bulosan. The Dunstan persona of "The Filipino Houseboy," we must remember, is an American whose novel was acquired by a movie studio in Hollywood and who ended up signing a five-year contract with that studio as a writer with a steady source of income, enough at least to afford such Hollywood trappings as Filipino houseboys. (He in fact gets the services of two for the price of one, since Conrado's cousin stays with them while jobless.)

Now, if we consider that Bulosan once dreamed of writing for television[9] but may have been blacklisted in Hollywood during the Red-baiting McCarthy years because of his political leanings,[10] and that Bulosan never had a steady source of income and could certainly not afford to hire servants, we realize that pseudonyms like Dunstan Peyton and Cecilio Baroga were, in Bulosan's time and circumstances, more than just authorial conceits because the rules of the publishing game exacted certain concessions from those who, out of necessity, worked within these rules. For Bulosan faced both racial and political discrimination in pursuit of his literary ambitions in America. If he initially made his name as a Filipino writer, his identity as such also tended to ghettoize him. His leftwing politics made it necessary for him to write under an "American" nom de plume, yet at the same time it gave him an opportunity to write as if he were a white man.

This doubleness explains why the name "Carlos Bulosan" does not appear on the manuscript of *Conspirators*. At the same time, this doubleness equally haunts the name "Dunstan Peyton," which represents the ironic flip side of Carlos Bulosan's persona, a deconstruction of the American dream. Dunstan's success story encapsulates the bitter truth of racism that Bulosan so movingly and angrily writes about in *America Is in the Heart*. In a sense, Dunstan's success would have been Carlos', if Carlos had been a white man living in America. Something of the poignancy that comes across in Bulosan's creation of a white American persona based on facts, events, and projections from his own life resonates in a letter that he wrote to one of his friends. In the letter, Bulosan talks about wanting to "do something of great significance to the future of the islands [i.e., the Philippines]."[11] He proceeds to outline the plot of a novel "that concerns racial relations between Pinoys and white Americans," racial relations that also have a specifically sexual inflection via the tragedy of miscegenation. Let us quote the passage in its entirety:

> Suddenly in the night a Filipino houseboy kills a friend and in his attempt to escape from the law he stumbles into his dark room and bumps into the wall. When he wakes up he is confronted by a veiled image in the darkness who reveals to him that he has become white. It is true, of course, that he has become a white man. But the image tells him that he will remain a white man so long as he will not fall in love with a white woman! Then, according to the warning of the image, he would become a Filipino again, ugly, illiterate, monster-like, and vicious.
>
> This is a parable, of course, an American parable. Some elements in America gave us a gift of speech, education, money, but they also wanted to take away our heart. They give you money but deny your humanity. So this is the great challenge to the protagonist of the novel: to give up the opportunity of being a white man who is intelligent, moneyed and also hand-

some, to become an ugly Filipino again in order to follow the tragic course of his heart—his love for a white
woman—this is the theme. He was a white man for
three days in the book; then he becomes a Filipino again.
There was no use living a lie anyway. For one thing, he
had killed a good friend; there was no choice. But the
murder is secondary to the racial issue; that America
denies our humanity.

One is tempted to read, in Bulosan's use of the allegory
of the white man and of the brown man's love for the white
woman, more than just the anguish of the brutalized native
who sees himself in and through the eyes of his oppressor, more, perhaps, than a bitter indictment of racism. Dunstan Peyton, whether
the persona of a text or the actual pseudonym of Bulosan, signi-
fies by its very existence as a name a condensation of many of
Bulosan's recurring concerns, as well as his own self-allegorizing as
a Filipino writer working in racist America.

The doubleness of Bulosan's self-identification can also
be seen in *Conspirators'* recurring motif of "passing." One of the
fantasies that is played out by the novel's American characters is
that of going "native." This fantasy brings into play a combination of attraction and repulsion, observation and participation,
and proximity and distance on the part of the white sojourner/
traveler. It is exemplified by Gar Stanley's Noble-Savage affinity
for the Igorots, who are likened to the American Indians, and
it recalls the White Apos of the highlands during the American
period. This fantasy is a gendered one, moreover, since women
like Candy and Tampa are apparently immune to the allure of
the Noble Savage and his way of life, although this does not stop
them from donning "native" disguises in order to escape detec-
tion by their respective enemies. Both Gar and Tampa speak local
languages with some fluency. Conversely, the fair-skinned and
blue-eyed Pepe Gonzales, who turns out to be a bona fide agent
of the Philippine state, acquits himself in Gar's eyes during a
hands-only Igorot dinner by mixing with his Igorot hosts.

Read in this context, *All the Conspirators* demands the kind
of reading that takes into account the conflictive elements in
Bulosan's ideological positions. The novel itself enacts this

conflict on the levels of narrative and theme. On the one hand, the reader is asked to assume the point of view of an American who grew up in the Philippines and whose father, an engineer-turned-businessman, benefited directly from American colonial rule and its imposition of parity rights for Americans regarding the exploitation of mineral resources in the Philippines. On the other hand, this American, sympathetic to the plight of the oppressed, also appears intimately connected to "home," to the seemingly alien landscape and its inhabitants.

That the rich mestizo Pepe ends up being revealed as one of the "good guys" would, moreover, appear to upset our reading of Bulosan as a critic of neocolonialism and racism. But then so would the fact that a white American, William Pomeroy, could be a high-ranking member of the first Philippine communist party. We might also object to Bulosan's positive portrayal of the government's role in catching the collaborators, given that the issue of collaboration in real life implicated politicians like Manuel Roxas, who went on to become the first elected president of the postwar Philippines. This is probably the aesthetic equivalent of Bulosan's almost rhapsodic account of his interaction with Commonwealth president Manuel L. Quezon.[12] If we are to give a nuanced reading of Bulosan, we would have to account not just for his radical ideas but also for the way in which these ideas coexisted with nostalgic evocations of Quezon.

One of the interesting things about *Conspirators* is that it sets itself up as a conventional thriller, with the protagonist "getting the girl" (here, the relatively unscathed Tampa, who survives her father's assassination) and emerging from his adventure with only a few bruises or broken bones. But it does so only to undermine the conventions of that thriller in the end. The main protagonist in most thrillers gets to the heart of the mystery, and extracts from his adventures the revelation of which he is the catalyst. The ideal hero is the detective, who constructs a correct account out of the pieces of the puzzle. No matter that he is caught unaware or subjected to perils. The reader is made to feel that the danger somehow follows from, and often constitutes the fitting climax to, the protagonist's discovery of the truth.

But in this novel, the only thing that Stanley discovers at the end of the novel is Candy's treachery and his own unwitting complicity as Candy's dupe. Pepe and the state arrive just in time to save Stanley from getting the bullet himself and ending up as just one of the many hapless victims whose corpses litter the text. But the main exposition, which gestures toward a wider network of non-overlapping surveillance and collaboration extending beyond Stanley's personal connection with the ring, makes us rethink Goyo's statement about the putative recipient of the ring. Was the ring really meant for Stanley? Could it have been "really" intended for Pepe and the state? Or perhaps more suggestively, was it actually meant as a death warrant for Candy and the other collaborators?

In a way, we are reminded of the centrality of the web motif in *The Cry and the Dedication*, which follows seven Huk rebels as they travel across the postwar Philippine landscape for a Manila rendezvous with a Filipino from America who bears much needed succor for the resistance movement. Each of the seven characters has been chosen for the mission because of his or her ability to provide one piece that adds up to the bigger picture of the mission, although none of them, not even their charismatic leader Hassim, knows the full details. Some of the members have been chosen for their specialized knowledge of the different places through which the band will pass. Old Bio, for example, successfully steers the band through the forest surrounding his hometown. Others are equipped to provide a crucial service in ensuring the mission's success in locating and positively identifying the man from America. Only Dante, a Filipino sojourner from America, knows what the contact person looks like. And only Mameng, the lone female member of the mission, can confirm that the contact person is truly Felix Rivas, the activist who had been physically emasculated by American vigilantes in California.

Like *The Cry and the Dedication*, the web of interconnection in *Conspirators* links characters from different sections of Philippine society. The main difference is that in *Conspirators*, the connections have a more pronounced contingency about them because the characters are neither united nor disciplined nor, ultimately, ennobled by a sense of mission and self-sacrifice. *Conspirators'* history is history in its most arbitrary sense, history as happenstance and coincidence without the redeeming promise of coherent meaning. The pattern that emerges out of chaos is that of chance connections rather than concerted action. Street-smart Goyo, for example, basically, operates on his own while serving as the main conduit for Stanley's encounter with the Igorot Damyan, who, unknown to Goyo, actually works with Pepe Gonzales.

Although collaborator and non-collaborator alike are looking for the owner of the ring, they are propelled in different directions by different, but often overwhelmingly selfish and venal motives. This novel asks what it would be like if the Brownian movement of these myopic representatives of the different strata of society collided. The results, as we well know, can be as explosive and barbaric as the brutal struggles then taking place in Manila. The key "mission" in the novel is aborted when the commando from whom Clem was supposed to obtain the much needed money to finance the guerilla warfare is killed by the collaborators, and Clem himself is wounded by the Japanese and later finished off by the collaborators.

Cry ends with the death of Dante, also known as Conrado Bustamante, the only man who can identify the expatriate who awaits the band at the meeting point. The Huk mission to the city is therefore exposed to the same contingencies and risks as those faced by Gar Stanley. But we get the sense that, in Cry, losing one battle does not decisively tip the scales in the enemy's favor because there will be other missions and other battles. For the novel suggests that it is History itself that impels events and characters forward, the latter often to their deaths.

This History recuperates the contingencies of the characters' everyday struggles and reinvests them with the affective and intellectual charge of nationalist solidarity. The characters in Cry are "Filipinos" representing different sectors of society, fellow conspirators who, despite their varied individual histories and personal ties, are united in their struggle against oppression and in their vision of a better Philippines. But they are also "national" in that they not only move across space, but cut across the "natural" barriers of language as well. Hassim, for example, was born in Bicol but grew up in Tondo and speaks perfect Tagalog. Dabu is Ilocano but speaks good Panggalatok, Linda Bie is Visayan and speaks Spanish at home. Dante writes in English and speaks Pampango, among other languages.

What is interesting about the Filipinoness of these characters is that it is not really defined in terms of a hierarchy of native languages. Bulosan, after all, was an Ilocano who emigrated to the U.S. during the early thirties, a time when English was the privileged language of instruction and government and the identification of Filipino nationalism with a Tagalog-based but putatively hybrid "Pilipino" (metamorphosing during the past decade into "Filipino") lay well in the future. Like Rizal and Mabini, Bulosan wrote in the language of the enemy. In a sense, he assumed that it was the content, more than the vehicle or medium, of the text which mattered as far as expressing sociopolitical ideas were concerned. His novels did not register the effects of the much later expansion of the commercial media and the efforts of both official and anti-state nationalism to create self-consciously language-based political and cultural frameworks for articulating nationness during the sixties and seventies.

It may, of course, be argued that Hassim, the leader, speaks Tagalog. But Hassim leads the mission precisely because his Tagalog serves a specific purpose for the Manila mission, not because Tagalog is the defining attribute of his leadership. In fact, his ability to speak the local dialect of Old Bio's hometown is as crucial to the mission as his fluency in Tagalog. Bulosan's vision suggests that the unhierarchical coexistence of many languages, including "foreign" tongues like English and Spanish, does not pose a threat to the nation's solidarity and unity of purpose. Neither is it an impediment to political pedagogy. Such a vision will today seem strange for those who believe that a single "national language" is the sine qua non of a "national culture," and for whom English and Spanish have been irreparably contaminated by colonial elitism. We tend to lose sight of this particular aspect of Bulosan's complexity as a writer if we view him and his work solely through the prism of our time, a time when Filipinoness has come to be intimately conjoined, if not often conflated, with linguistic hierarchy. Bulosan's sanguine depiction of multilingual political action would no doubt have confused even the seasoned "Father of the Philippine National Language," Manuel L. Quezon, who invoked political and semantic transparency, that is, the fear of (mis)translation, as the *raison d'etre* for a single national language:

I never realized how terrible the lack of common language is until I became President. I am President of the Philippines; I am the personal representative of the Philippine nation, the Philippine people. But, when I travel through the provinces and talk to my people, I need an interpreter. Did you ever hear of anything more humiliating, more horrible than that? I am all right when I go to the Tagalog provinces, because I can speak to the people there in the vernacular. But if I go to Ilocos Sur, I am already a stranger in my own country! How can I tell the people what I think and feel when in order to do so I need an interpreter who, in the majority of cases, says what he wants to say and not what I have said? That happens because sometimes the interpreter, either because he has not understood me or because he cannot think of words in the vernacular expressing what I have said, says whatever occurs to him. How often have I not said to someone interpreting for me in Visayan or Bicol: "You are not saying what I have said?"[13]

Quezon's demand for a common language appears eminently logical until the reader asks how, given his avowal of the irreducible risks of mistranslation, Quezon could have, nevertheless, sufficiently ascertained that he was being misquoted by his interpreter for the latter to merit one of the former's famous tongue-lashings.

But the pros and cons of translation notwithstanding, *Cry* offers us a remarkable and inspiring account of solidarity and resistance against the depredations of neocolonialism in general, an account that seeks to link activists in America and in other countries to the struggle for national liberation "back home." On the home front, the Huk rebels are even aided by a non-Huk band. The possibilities of reciprocal aid and of solidarity are endless. Even Dante manages to achieve an epiphany regarding his doubleness as an "American" and a "Filipino," a doubleness that he now experiences as a "fusion of his two selves," a "bridge at long last, spanning the chasm between the two lives which he had lived."

This inspiring vision of reconciled selves and divisions, however, is deeply marked by an awareness of just how fragile the vision is. Drawn to "the native land" by a sense of responsibility,[14] Dante realizes that the risk that one incurs by dying for an idea may be, as Hassim observed, that of leaving no other reminders of oneself in the world save that of having fought and made the ultimate sacrifice for that idea. Here is Hassim in that moment of realization:

> Soon he, Hassim, would be dead too; and nothing would remain to remind the world that he had fought and died for an idea. Was it better to die for an idea than live without any? Dante had the idea to recreate the lost folklore of his country. Has he died for it? Hassim could not know; he would never know. Time was the element; and then he sighed, so great was his burden that for a moment he was tempted to shout at the coming sun.

Hassim realizes that no sacrifice, however ultimate or absolute, can guarantee the patriot's claim to immortality because, although it proceeds from the ethical imperative to realize a better world, an insistence on "believing that a better world will emerge from our harsh and chaotic one," such a sacrifice necessarily entails not only the risk of dying, like Filipino national hero Jose Rizal's Elias, without seeing the dawn, but that of dying, like the many who remain nameless and outside history, without being remembered by those who do (or do not) see the dawn.

But if time is, indeed, the one element we must concede in our most cherished and concerted actions, it does not necessarily lead to a debilitating despair, nor does it vitiate the imperative of struggling against oppression:

> But he [Hassim] said to his companions, "Let us get going."
> "Go ahead," Rene [a non-Huk leader] said. "In case you are in these parts and in need of help ask for Rene."
> "We will do that," Hassim said.

They shook hands.
"God be with you!"
"Same to you!"
Hassim and his companions departed, and walked
into the new morning.

Hassim's "but" is not a mere gesture of defiance against time, but an instinctive recognition, finally, that the element of time to which we surrender our future also gives us the possibility and promise of that future. The promise is nothing less than the possibility of "the new morning," of history itself. Seen in this light, the most convincing proof of *All the Conspirators'* authenticity may be the fact that it is more than just a somber flipside of Bulosan's great novel; it is, instead, a photographic negative of *The Cry and the Dedication*, and must therefore be read alongside *Cry*, because both novels map, respectively, the corrosive and transformative truth of the neocolonial Philippines in all its manifestations, mutations, and possibilities.

CAROLINE S. HAU
BENEDICT ANDERSON

# Notes

[1]Among the book-length works on Bulosan that have appeared over the last thirty years are E. San Juan, *Carlos Bulosan and the Imagination of the Class Struggle* (Quezon City: University of the Philippines Press, 1972); P.C. Morantte, *Remembering Carlos Bulosan: His Heart Affair with America* (Quezon City: New Day Publishers, 1984); and Susan Evangelista, *Carlos Bulosan and His Poetry: A Biography and Anthology* (Quezon City: Ateneo de Manila University Press, 1985).

[2]Bulosan to Florentino B. Valeros, 8 April 1955, Carlos Bulosan Papers, University of Washington Libraries, p.1.

[3]Evangelista, *Carlos Bulosan and His Poetry*, p.1.

[4]See Licerio Lagda, "Introduction," *The Power of Money and Other Stories by Carlos Bulosan* (Manila: Kalikasan Press, 1990), p.7.

[5]Bulosan to Florentino B. Valeros, 8 April 1955, p. 2. The University of Washington Libraries does not have the third page of this letter. Excepts from page three are reprinted in Dolores Feria, ed., *Sound of Falling Light: Letters in Exile* (Quezon City; n.p., 1960), p. 86.

[6]Epifanio San Juan, Jr., "Introduction," *The Cry and the Dedication* (Philadelphia: Temple University Press, 1994), pp. ix and endnote number 1 on xxxiii. "As far as I can gather, there is only a passing allusion to this novel, referred to in his letters as *The Hounds of Darkness* (Bulosan 1960: 274)" (p. ix). San Juan bases his dating of the novel on this allusion: "I would strongly suggest that the book was begun sometime in 1952 or 1953 and was completed in 1955 when, in a letter to Florentino Valeros, Bulosan first mentioned the early title of this novel, *The Hounds of Darkness* (Bulosan 1960:274)" (p. xxxiii). Licerio Lagda puts Josephine Patrick's dating of *All the Conspirators* at 1952-1955, or roughly the same estimates advanced by San Juan for *The Cry and the Dedication*. Writes Lagda: "The typescript of the novel *All the Conspirators* in my possession is a carbon copy. Ms. Patrick believes that the novel was written in Seattle between 1952 and 1955. She thinks the original was submitted to Bulosan's literary agent under the pen name Dunstan Peyton." From p. 1 of a photocopy of Licerio Lagda's notes on *All the Conspirators*, Bulosan also used a Los Angeles P.O. Box number as his return address in at least two other stories. "The Return of the Amorous Ghost" and "Land of the Midnight Sun."

[7]The undated letter to Josephine Patrick does not have a clearly defined beginning or end and is unsigned. The "April 15, 1955" inscription on the upper right-hand corner is the archivist's dating. Bulosan to Josephine Patrick, 15 April 1955, Carlos Bulosan Papers, University of Washington Libraries.

[8]Bulosan's fondness for recycling his favorite titles is evident in a short story that he wrote entitled "The Cry and the Dedication." Like *Conspirators*, the narrator of "Cry" is a white man, this time a Scandinavian named Olaf, who befriends the learned Dr. Max Nado, a pariah who endures the abuse and vilification of the townspeople in lifelong atonement for the sins of his forefathers. The manuscript of "The Cry and the Dedication" can be found in the University of Washington Libraries.

[9]From Licerio Lagda's interview with Josephine Patrick. Cited in a photocopy of Licerio Lagda's notes on four Bulosan plays, including "Laughter is Our Only Wealth" (adapted from "My Father Goes to Court" in the *Laughter of My Father*) and "The Ghost on Alpine Street" (adapted from "The Amorous Ghost," which later appeared in *The Philippines Is in the Heart*). Bulosan apparently changed the Filipino characters in "The Amorous Ghost" to Americans in "The Ghost on Alpine Street." The main characters are Ann Garth and Mr. and Mrs. Garth.

[10]This information is provided by Susan Evangelista in *Carlos Bulosan and His Poetry*, p. 22: "Both Carlos Bulosan and his brother Aurelio believed that Carlos had been 'blacklisted' in Hollywood, and that is why he could not get work there." Evangelista also cites a University of Washington tape recording in which Bulosan's friend, activist Chris Mensalvas, refers to another Bulosan associate John Fante who claimed that "he (Fante) was barred from working at MGM because of his association with Carlos."

[11]Carlos Bulosan, Letter to Jose de los Reyes, April 17, 1947, in *Sound of Falling Light*, p. 47.

[12]See Carlos Bulosan, Letter to Grace F. Cunningham, August 1, 1944, in *Sound of Falling Light*, pp. 21-23. San Juan's reaction can be found in his *Carlos Bulosan and the Imagination of the Class Struggle*, pp.115-16.

[13]From Manuel L. Quezon's speech delivered at the San Juan de Letran Alumni Annual Banquet, San Juan de Letran College, Manila, November 7,

1937. Reprinted in *President Quezon and His Biographical Sketch, Messages and Speeches: A Record of the Progress and Achievement of the Philippine People*, edited by Eulogio B. Rodriguez (Manila: Publishers Incorporated, 1940), p. 151.

[14]Bulosan himself continued to be interested in developments in the Philippine literary and political scene. *Cry*, for example, draws on Luis Taruc's *Born of the People* and uses the actual *noms de guerre* of Huk leaders.

# EDITOR'S NOTE

I have tried to preserve the flavor of Bulosan's prose by retaining the language that he used in its original phrasing. The two substantive corrections (pages 31 and 143) are indicated by brackets, and the internal punctuation of the compound words has been edited to conform to conventional usage. Commas have been inserted, where necessary, into some sentences for the convenience of the readers. I have also edited "The Filipino Houseboy" to make it conform to Bulosan's handwritten corrections regarding the narrative persona of the story. I thank Judith Henchy of the University of Washington Libraries for her invaluable help in locating and crosschecking the materials used in this book.

C.S.H.

# ALL THE CONSPIRATORS

# ONE

It may be that one of these days I will return Stateside again. Maybe I will see once more the throat-tugging beauty of the Golden Gate Bridge and pass by the green shoulders of the Marin Hills to the docks of San Francisco, the Embarcadero, the cable cars, the strikes, the ten-cent stores and the paved streets. Maybe I will go back to a country where a man is reasonably sure of dying in bed and his life expectancy is determined by statistics and not another man's fancy.

I don't know.

Two months ago I did not expect to be here in Manila, though I had been born and spent my early life here. Way back in 1912, before I was born, Dad had come out here as a mining engineer. He fell in love with the town and then sent for his best girl in Chio. They were married in Manila and somehow, before Dad realized it, he had prospered quite easily and become part owner of a gold mine. Then the years melted away and he and Mother never returned to the United States.

That was why I did not see the United States until I went to Columbia University. While I was away my girl Candy married my best friend Clem Mayo. Then, the year I graduated, the real riot broke loose. War came and I was inducted into the army. The last news from Manila announced that my parents had been killed. Afterwards, when the fighting was finally over there seemed nothing to go back to that was worthwhile. Clem had also died in the war.

Maybe I could have eventually learned to like my postwar job with a shipping broker. But there was a great restlessness inside of me, a deep longing for the land where I grew up, the easy-going friendly people across the wide Pacific. Maybe it would have worked out if I had settled in an inland city.

But in Frisco, surrounded on three sides by the wistful invitation of swishing, churning waters, with ships honking insistently as they passed through the harbour, I couldn't keep my thoughts on manifests and bills of lading and all the other trivia that make up a shipping broker's day.

And even when I was on the roof garden of the gay Mark Hopkins I would forget my office companions, and my eyes would seek beyond the shoreline. I would see, not the long resplendent sweep of the mahogany bar and the sleek glossy women, but the luxuriant rows of coconut trees that lined Dewey Boulevard here in Manila, the rounded curve of the bay with the gray hump of Corregidor in the distance, and Candy and Clem and myself catching jellyfish in the so-blue water.

I was, you might say, in that mood where I was unconsciously looking for a good excuse to pack my bags and take off. So when I received the letter from Candy begging me to help her, it didn't take me long to make up my mind. For the sake of stuffy pride, though, I tried to kid myself for a few days that her problem had nothing to do with me. Yet all the time my mind kept reverting to her letter and I found myself re-reading it in the middle of office routine, and each time I read it I was caught up in the same mood as when I had first taken it from the envelope.

Her letter had struck me like a warm sweet breath of sampaguita one particularly dreary morning when the wind holed down the canyons of Market Street and the air was mournful with the promise of faraway rain.

"Dear Gar," Candy wrote, "I am in trouble and need you. I have just received conclusive evidence that Clem is still alive. I want to find him, but I need your assistance. Please help me."

That was the whole letter. No explanations. There was no apparent concern on her part that she was asking me to toss away a lucrative, though dull, job. But that was Candy.

Before the war, none of us had given much thought to money. Clem and I had always been at Candy's beck and call. And Clem, being the older, was just a little quicker at jockeying himself into first place in her interests. Except for one interval when Clem was nineteen and fell in love with a warm-eyed French girl from Shanghai and married her. Candy was fifteen then. She could not understand Clem's sudden switch from pulling her pigtails to making love to someone else.

Clem's marriage did not last long, however. His French wife died a year later in childbirth, leaving Clem, at twenty, a widower and the father of a daughter, who was later named Tampa. Of course, with these events behind him, he was far too mature for Candy and me. He ignored us both for months. It was during this period that Candy became my girl, and when, two years later, I left for New York, it was understood that she would be waiting for me.

But a girl of seventeen in the tropics is ripe for marriage. And youth being what it is everywhere, Candy did not wait. I was gone less than a year when she married Clem. I was very much disappointed and tried to console myself with the material I found at hand, and several times I thought I had succeeded. Even after the war and I heard Clem was dead, I would not go back. I told myself that one burn was enough. But I knew that what I was really waiting for was an invitation from Candy.

All these thoughts came to my mind when I read Candy's brief letter. As I say, I stuck to my guns for a few days. But all the while I was quitting my job, packing, getting my visa, and arranging to take the first available plane. I told myself that, after all, there was Clem to consider. He had been like my old brother. And if I owed nothing to Candy, there was still Clem's daughter.

So here I was, back in Manila for the first time in fourteen years. While the plane circled and swooped to the airport, it seemed incredible that I had been away so long. But a little later, as I drove into town, I realized that war had passed this way and left this once gay city a mass of crumpling ruins. Everywhere I looked, I could see skeletons of buildings and torn streets and tottering walls.

I told the cab driver to go down Taft Avenue where our house had been. But when I passed through it, my heart was heavy. The fine homes that had lined Taft and Pennsylvania were all burned to ashes. Now you could see makeshift contraptions of corrugated iron, packing boxes and bits of charred wood, held together by God knows what. These are called barong-barongs and are inhabited by squatters.

4

One block over on exclusive Dewey Boulevard the fine apartment houses were gone, and so were the coconut trees that had lined it. Now you could see Manila Bay clearly, where stumps of sunken ships stuck up out of the water, telltale signs of a war that was desperately fought. I couldn't believe this destruction although I had been told about it.

I had gone through the war like an automaton, doing what I was told. Not liking it, I also did not feel much about it.

And now I was home. And suddenly I felt as if I were going to war for the first time. For the first time I was suddenly aware of that living hate which is supposed to be necessary in a soldier. But my hate was directed against the forces that had made this destruction necessary and had wrought so much suffering to millions of people. It kindled in me a grim determination to do whatever I could for Clem. The suffering of Manila had been Clem's suffering too, and whether he was living or dead I would see this thing through.

After I had seen as much desolation as I could stand I finally told the driver to take me to the address Candy had given me. I wondered if she, too, were living in one of these makeshift huts. And I found it hard to imagine her living in an atmosphere of poverty.

I lolled back in the cab trying to recall Candy as she had looked when I last saw her. She had been a slim long-legged girl of seventeen, with hair so blonde it was almost like silver and a skin deeply tanned by the tropical sun. But what I remembered most were her lips, small and full, that always lingered between a pout and a smile, and her eyes, heavy-lidded and sleepy-looking, even when she laughed. She had a flowerlike face that every boy dreams about. That was how Clem and I had nicknamed her Candy.

In a way I dreaded this first moment of meeting, afraid of what I might find. I told myself not to expect the Candy I had grown up with, the sweet and spoiled youngster of my youth who managed to make you like it even when she was getting her own way. Fourteen years is a long time, and she had been through the ravages of war and tragedy.

The car swung left off Dewey Boulevard and stopped. I stared in amazement. I consulted the address again. There was no mistake. This was the number she had given me.

5

I got out of the car looking with wonder at the pink plaster dwelling built behind a trim, well-kept lawn. This district was completely untouched by the destruction. I told the driver to wait.

I pressed the bell and listened to the answering chime. Then the door opened and there stood Candy herself.

Candy and I stared at each other for a few seconds in silence while fourteen years surged up between us like a mighty wave and then settled slowly around our feet.

"Mrs. Mayo, I presume?" I grinned.

Candy found her voice. "Oh, Gar," she said, pulling me inside. "Gar, you've become so handsome. But I'd still know you anywhere by your ears."

I involuntarily touched my right ear. My ears had always stood out just a little. They had been a sensitive point when I was growing up, probably because Candy had always teased me about them.

"A fine homecoming," I said, shutting the door. "All you can remember about me is my ears!"

Suddenly she threw her arms around me and her soft light head lay against my shoulder. "Oh, Gar," she whispered, "I missed you and I need you so much."

Then I knew the reason why I had returned. I knew it wasn't only for Clem and Tampa. I knew that even if I had been in South Africa one word from Candy would have brought me to her.

I kissed her and held her off so I could look at her.

"Smile at me, Candy," I said, "Smile. I want to see all your wrinkles."

She made a face and whirled around. "Do I look very middle-aged?" she teased.

"You look younger than when I left," I said.

It was almost true. Candy was still Candy. Still the girl with the face that belonged on a box of chocolates. Her hair was still incredibly light and fine and it framed her neck and shoulders in shimmering waves. The only difference was in her eyes. They were wider now, not nearly as sleepy-looking, but the effect only made her younger and more mysterious.

"Why didn't you cable me when to expect you?" she pouted, drawing me into the sala. "I would have met you."

6

"I wanted to surprise you," I said. "I didn't even wait to check in at a hotel."

"You'll stay here, of course," said Candy. She waved her arm around. "I've plenty of room. Besides, since the war you can't get a room to yourself even at the Manila Hotel."

She didn't have to twist my arm to accept that invitation.

"I'll believe anything about Manila after what I've seen today," I said.

"Poor Gar," said Candy softly. "I forgot it would be a shock to you. Did you see your old home?"

I nodded. "Is all the city like this?"

"Not all," she said. "The worst fighting was down here. But you see damaged buildings in every district." She sighed. "I'm tired of talking about the war. I want to forget it."

I patted her shoulder. She was still a little girl.

"I'll cheer you up in no time. Happy Gar. That's me. Wait here till I get my luggage."

I paid off the driver outside and carried my bags into the house.

I followed the maid up the stairs that led to a balcony over the sala. The guest room was not large like the older houses. But it might have been copied from a Hollywood movie scene. Everything was smart and cool and comfortable. No horrors of war here. I was glad, for Candy's sake. And mine too, temporarily.

I told Candy so when I rejoined her downstairs.

"Yes, I am lucky," Candy said. "Clem's father built this house for us as a wedding gift. Since the war, I remodeled the rest into apartments." She smiled a little sadly. "And I'm not getting rich. Prices in Manila now are out of this world." Her tone brightened when the maid came in with glasses and bottles on a tray. "Here is something you haven't had in ages—real San Miguel Beer!"

I emptied half a glass of the beer at a gulp, savoring the cool bittersweetness of it on my tongue.

"Ah," I said, "this is what I came home for."

"Is it indeed?" pouted Candy. "I thought it was to see me."

I pulled her hand and leaned back contentedly against the cushions.

7

"Candy and beer," I amended. "And Clem."

"Yes, of course," she said quietly. "You want to hear about Clem." She took a little breath and got up. She went to a drawer and unlocked it. She returned holding an object. "Do you remember this?"

I looked at the object. It was a man's ring made of bronze, fashioned with delicate workmanship. It was engraved with tiny scrolls that represented the sun's rays. This type of ring is made only by the Igorots in the mountain country of Northern Luzon. As I stared at the ring a flood of memories poured over me. I remembered this ring well. I had it made especially for Clem years before, when we were on a hunting trip in the Igorot mountains.

I turned the ring over and looked inside the band. Sure enough, the inscription was there: "G.S. to C.M. 1935".

I looked up at Candy. Her eyes were moist. "Clem always wore that ring," she said. "In fact, after he put on weight, he could not get it off. He was wearing it when I last saw him. It was impossible for anyone to steal it from him, unless it was filed off his finger."

I looked at the ring again. There was no mark or scratch of any kind on the band.

"I don't understand it," I said.

"Only Clem could have removed that ring," said Candy. "And then only if he became thin enough to take it off himself."

I turned the ring over and over in my hand.

"Tell me all about it," I said. "How did you get it?"

Candy lit a cigarette and sat down beside me.

"I'll tell you the whole story," she said.

# TWO

"I will start from the beginning," said Candy, sipping her beer. "We had all been expecting war for several months. We had, accordingly, closed our house in Manila and moved to the summer place that Clem's family owned in Baguio. You remember it, don't you?"

I did indeed. All I had to do was close my eyes and see again that great white house with the pink marble terrace overlooking the pine-covered mountainside. In my boyhood days I had attended Brent, the American school in Baguio, and spent most of my vacations with Clem and his family. I nodded my head now and Candy continued.

"Clem joined the Army. He was in the terrible retreat on Bataan. But when word came that Wainwright was going to surrender, Clem and several others decided to escape and join the guerillas. I don't know how he ever made his way back clear across Luzon to Baguio. It took him almost three months." A shadow flitted across her face. Then she went on in a steady voice. "I had already left Baguio, of course. The Japs by that time had rounded up all the Americans for the concentration camps. To escape concentration I had joined a Filipino family and we had gone into hiding in the mountains. Clem finally found us there."

"What about Clem's youngster, Tampa?" I interrupted.

Candy nodded. "I forgot to mention that I had Tampa with me. Then Clem appeared from somewhere and organized the natives into a guerilla unit. Gar, it was terrible living out there." Her voice suddenly broke down and she crept into my arms and hid her head for a minute against my shoulder. Drying her eyes she continued. "The unspeakable filth, the crude existence of those mountain people. They weren't even Christians. I thought I would go mad." She raised her face and looked at me with eyes that were clouded with tragic memory. "Can you understand, Gar? It's hard when you have been brought up with everything and then suddenly found yourself turned loose in an atmosphere as primitive as the American Indians. They eat only wild meat and grasses and roots and live in miserable little huts, and nothing matters to them except eating and sleeping and lusting. Can you understand how I felt?"

I patted her shoulder. I knew the Igorots of the mountains well. I had many friends among them. Years ago I had gone hunting and fishing and visiting in their villages. But it was different, of course, for men. A girl like Candy—well, Candy was a blossom, delicate and fragile as a jungle orchid. She had been born to wealth and all the luxury that the tropics bestows on the white man with means.

"What happened?" I asked.

She said. "I finally told Clem I couldn't stand it any longer. I told him I would give myself up and go into a concentration camp. At least I would have been among my friends." She smiled a little ruefully. "But Clem conceived a plan. He had my body stained dark brown so that I could pass for a native. I dyed my hair black. That's one thing the natives know: they have developed stains and dyes from roots and barks of trees. Then posing as a poor native, I went back to Baguio. I found that our house had been taken over by Jap officers. I knew enough about the native language to fool the officers. I still had no definite plan, but I secured a job in my own kitchen. But, as it turned out, it wasn't a real job. Our cook, Dayang, was still there. She recognized me but showed no sign of intimacy. She looked after me. Tampa was no problem. She was dark anyway—her mother was French, you know—and, being a youngster, she had picked up the mountain language in a few months."

Candy drained her glass of beer. I filled her glass while I waited for her to finish her story.

"Everything worked out well," continued Candy. "I secured a lot of information. Once a week Clem, disguised as a native, came to the market. I met him there and passed on what news I could. Then one day he told me that a commando was arriving from the United States. He was a Filipino soldier who had been landed by submarine and he was assigned to work in the mountains. He was to stop at our house and Clem would meet him there to guide him to the guerilla outpost. It was very dangerous to meet under the noses of the Japanese officers, but Clem took the risk."

"And then?"

"The commando arrived, but Clem did not show up. It was too dangerous to hide the commando, so Tampa started to lead him to Clem's camp. That was the last time I ever saw Tampa. But later I heard from the guerillas that Clem had set out to meet the commando and had been killed by the Japs on the way. The funny thing about it all is that the commando's body was found, but not those of Clem or Tampa. And another thing, the commando had on him thousands of American dollars to distribute among the guerillas. The money disappeared."

She stopped and looked at me as if to add significance to her last words. Then she leaned back wearily against the cushions and went on in low monotones as if she were telling a story that was meant only for herself.

"That is all I heard of Clem until a month ago when I was shopping in Manila. In a little shop off the Escolta that deals in jewelry and trinkets, I found this ring. I asked the shopowner where he purchased it, but he said that he had forgotten." She turned to me suddenly as if she had just remembered I was there. Her voice had a pleading quality. "This may not seem like much evidence to go on, yet I have a feeling that Clem is—or was, until recently—alive somewhere."

"But why wouldn't he come back himself?" I asked.

"Maybe he's afraid," said Candy.

"Afraid of what?" I asked sharply.

She shook her head. "Who knows? Maybe he has been injured so badly that he can't come. Maybe he can't explain about the death of the commando and why the money disappeared."

I was suddenly on my feet, shaking her by the shoulders.

"Candy!" I found myself shouting. "Do you know what you're saying?"

Candy lifted heavy blue-lidded eyes to me.

"Don't shout, Gar," she said. "I'm probably wrong. But—"
"She hesitated as if she were trying to find the right words. "—it's something inside that has always told me that Clem is not dead. If he is alive I want to find him. Please help me, Gar."

I stared at her for a moment.

"All right," I said finally. "I'll run this thing down. But let me tell you one thing. If Clem is alive he isn't hiding for any of the reasons at which you have been hinting. I know Clem like I know my own father. And he would never sell out."

"I don't care what he has done," said Candy. "The war is over and whatever he did, I know he must have a good explanation. Gar, help me so that once and for all I will know the whole truth."

I ran my fingers through her soft hair. I couldn't stay mad long at Candy.

"You know I'll help you, you witch," I said laughing. "You know you put a hex on me when I was seven and I've never gotten over it. But I'll tell you something." I raised her chin. "Don't expect too much. The trail is pretty cold by now. But I'll do what I can. Now, where is that shop where you found the ring?"

"You can't go there now," said Candy. "This is the siesta hour. Have you forgotten that at this time of day nobody raises a hand except to brush off a fly?"

Her words made me smile. I had forgotten that unlike the United States where business was promptly attended to, things over here were done in the slowest manner possible. I leaned forward now and raised my hand. But it was not to swat a fly. I poured myself another beer.

Just then the maid announced lunch. We ate in the cool screened-in dining room overlooking a tiny patio. The meal might have come from any average kitchen in the States: cold cuts, a huge salad, various cheeses and mountains of fresh bread, warm from the oven. In this atmosphere of plenty, enclosed by the little patio which was bright with scarlet flowers, thick green foliage and young banana trees, it was hard to believe that only a few blocks away the rest of the city lay heaped in a vast waste of destruction.

"There seems to be plenty of food in this land," I said, spreading a hunk of bread with a thick layer of soft tropical butter.

"You know how it is, Gar," said Candy. "If you have a friend you can get anything. An Army officer keeps me supplied from the PX. Otherwise, with prices the way they are, I'd have to go native and live on rice and fish."

While we were eating the maid announced a visitor. Candy made a sour face. Then she told the maid to show the caller into the dining room.

"A would-be suitor," whispered Candy. "He's nice, but he is a nuisance. Help me get rid of him." She looked up and smiled when the visitor appeared in the door. "Come in, Pepe," said Candy. "Please join us. This is Pepe Gonzales," she added to me. "His family has been selling real estate in Manila for three hundred years."

"Candy always makes that remark when she introduces me," said Pepe. "You'd think in three hundred years we could have bought the town ourselves."

He grinned and sat down. He seemed a nice guy. I liked him. He belonged to the young generation of mestizos who are seen everywhere in Manila, part native, part Spanish or American. In his case the blending was Spanish. He was slight of build but his eyes were blue and his complexion lighter and more smooth than any American in the tropics. In addition he lent his tropical whites an air of casual jauntiness—something no American is quite able to achieve.

"Gar Stanley," Pepe repeated, trying to remember. "I've heard of your father. You have a mine in Baguio, don't you?"

That is Manila for you. Everybody knows everybody else's father. Nobody can remain anonymous. And sometimes it is a little inconvenient.

"It was only half a mine," I said. "And I'm afraid now there isn't even that much left."

"Did you come back to reopen it?" asked Pepe.

"If it wasn't too badly damaged," I said. I caught Candy's quick glance in my direction. I could see that she did not want me to mention Clem. I, also, felt discretion was best until I found out more about Clem's disappearance. And there was no reason for Pepe to know that I was too broke to start the mine running again.

But he was discreet, too. He did not press the subject.

After lunch, Pepe suggested we all drive with him to visit his sister who lived in the new section of Quezon City.

"She has all the comforts of Beverly Hills," said Pepe. "A swimming pool, a badminton court, hot and cold running water."

"You and Candy can go," I said quickly, because I saw that Candy was on the point of refusing him. "I have an appointment. Business. I'll see you in the bar of the Manila Hotel later."

"You Americans," said Pepe. "Always rushing around to get business. You have been in the Philippines for half a century and still you haven't learned our formula for making money."

"What is that?" I asked.

"Inherit it, or marry it. Simple, and it always works," said Pepe.

I laughed. "I believe you have something there. I'll think it over."

Candy wasn't looking too happy. She had, I knew, expected to be with me. But this was a job I had to handle alone.

I said goodbye to them and hurried out before Pepe could offer to drive me.

I picked up a cruising cab on Dewey Boulevard and told the driver to drop me at the entrance to the Escolta. On the way, past the terrible ruins of the government buildings, I was again struck by the raw contrast between easy luxury and naked poverty in Manila.

I left the cab at the entrance to the Escolta. This was the first step of my search into the mystery surrounding Clem's disappearance. I found myself a little excited.

# THREE

The Escolta is the main shopping district in Manila. It is a narrow street, scarcely four blocks long, crowded on both sides with small shops, drugstores, restaurants, drygoods stores and a theatre. It is here that the well-to-do Filipinos and Americans do most of their shopping.

When I started down the sunbaked street the siesta hour was just over and the shops were beginning to open their doors again. I had forgotten Manila could be so hot. I was soaking wet. I wanted some beer. But I did not stop at any of the numerous bars and small counters that opened on the street. I hurried down towards the end of the Escolta as fast as the meandering crowds would allow me.

I turned right at the end of the Escolta. Here I was back again to the rubble of devastation. A ruined warehouse with one standing wall and the gutted eyes of blasted windows loomed up. Beneath the warehouse was a makeshift hovel of corrugated tin and packing boxes. A family of six squatted listlessly around the doorway. The family wash was hanging on a string across the street, dripping dirty water on unsuspecting passersby. Across the street was a small shop. The window displayed trinkets and jewelry, hand-painted wooden native slippers, handwoven mats and scarves. This was the place.

I went inside. The shop was cluttered up inside with the same items displayed in the windows. A couple of American women and Filipinas ambled around, looking at the wares. I stepped up to the counter. A young saleswoman suddenly appeared. She was typical of the younger generation, slim and clean-featured, with coils of black hair piled high on her head, and a slash of magenta lipstick brightening the light cocoa of her skin.

I asked for the owner.

"He is out," said the girl. "Perhaps I can help you."

I took the ring out of my pocket and showed it to her.

"I would like to know where this ring came from," I said.

A mask shadowed the friendly expression on her face.

"We don't deal in black market goods," she said quickly. "Everything here is shipped to us from America."

"Now look," I said quietly, "this ring did not come from America. It belonged to a friend of mine."

She snatched the ring from my hand and ran into the back room. I could hear voices speaking in Tagalog. I can understand the language, but their voices were pitched too low for me to catch the words. But I thought I understood the reason for her agitation. I had been too abrupt. I forgot the black market trade that was rampant in Manila. Docks and wharves were robbed by gangsters and thugs, who sold the stolen goods to the merchants and retail stores.

The curtain at the back parted and a man, apparently the owner, came towards me. He was a squat little man, baldish on top and thick around the belly. His heavy jowls and stolid expression indicated a considerable Chinese mixture in his veins. He stopped at the end of the counter and indicated with a jerk of his head that I was to follow him. We went to a dark corner.

"You bought this ring from me?" he asked softly.

"No, not exactly." I said. "This ring belonged to a friend of mine who I thought was killed in the war. But I have no wish to cause you trouble. I am only trying to trace him."

"My new jewelry," said the shopowner, "comes from America. But as you can see," he indicated the woven baskets and fiber tablecloths,"I also deal in native products. I also buy from peddlers and persons who have only a few pieces of jewelry left from the war."

"This is an unusual ring," I said. "Can't you remember where it came from?"

A gleam of interest lit his eyes, but he did not answer. Then I remembered. The only thing that talks in Manila is a five-peso bill. I pulled one from my pocket and let the end of it show between my fingers.

"This ring was made especially for my friend," I said. "There is no other one like it. I am very anxious to find him."

The shopowner looked at the money. Then he looked at me. He put back the ring in my palm.

"I'm afraid you have made a mistake," he said. "This ring was not bought here. Yes, it is an unusual piece. I will give you a good price for it."

"I don't want to sell it," I said irritably. "I'm trying to find out—"

"You have made a mistake," he said. He bowed slightly, retreating to the curtained doorway. "Good afternoon."

I swung away from the counter, baffled and angry. I strode towards the street entrance and collided with a man standing inside the door. I knocked his hat off. I picked it up and mumbled a hasty apology. I briefly noticed that he was wearing an old black alpaca suit. There were dark pockmarks on his chin. I rushed outside.

The midafternoon heat was stifling. I did not go back to the Escolta. Instead I wandered down the next street, picking my way through rubble and rocks, past a building that seemed ready to fall down any minute.

I couldn't figure out what had happened in the trinket shop. Something about the ring was definitely mysterious and ominous. At one point in our conversation, the proprietor was about to talk, then suddenly clammed up. I had either said too much or too little. He had refused my money, but he had offered to buy the ring. That was not like a shopowner in Manila.

As I trudged along I noticed that I was the only one on the street. Everybody else had dived for shelter out of the heat. I decided to do the same before I had sunstroke. I looked for a place where I could get some beer. A carromata rattled past, pulled by a bony horse.

Then the street was suddenly quiet. All at once I had a funny sensation that someone was behind me. There was a sound of a rolling rock, as if someone's foot had inadvertently slipped on it. I looked around. And I had the feeling that someone had just stepped out of sight. I stepped into a doorway and found myself at the beer place. I went in and sat down at the bar, turning so that I could keep an eye on the street.

The place was just a joint, the kind of dive found on a waterfront in any port city. It wasn't screened, it wasn't cool, it wasn't even clean. Flies and cockroaches clung on the walls. A couple of sailors huddled at the other end of the counter. Beside them stood the barmaid, a young girl with long stringy hair and a dirty dress. She lazily waved a crumpled newspaper in the air, swatting at flies that threatened customers' glasses.

A small figure in black alpaca darted through the open door and sat down beside me.

"How about a drink?" asked the newcomer.

I looked at him sharply. He was the fellow whose hat I had knocked off in the trinket shop. So it was Pock Marks who had been following me.

"Why should I?" I said.

"I hear you are interested in rings," he said in a low voice.

"Two beers," I said to the bartender.

"I'll have a whiskey chaser," said Pock Marks. "I don't always beg for drinks," he said with a grin. "But these are hard times and I have to pick up a little where I can. Salud!" He downed the whiskey in one gulp and started on the beer.

I took the ring from my pocket and held it out to him.

"What do you know about this?" I asked.

He almost spilled his beer.

"Put that away," he said. "You never know who's watch-ing." He regarded me sharply. "You are new at this game, aren't you?"

"I'm all at sea," I confessed honestly. "I'm only trying to locate a pal of mine."

I had given the bartender a ten-peso bill. The change lay on the counter. Pock Marks reached over and picked up a five.

"Okay?" he asked, grinning.

I nodded. He put the bill in his pocket and sipped his beer. "To begin with," he said, wiping the foam off his lips, "you must be careful what questions you ask and who you ask them to. There is much more to this ring business than you think. Don't forget: the war may be over but not the terror." He finished his beer and rapped on the counter for another. All this time his eyes did not leave mine. "Are you afraid of your neck?" he asked.

"Good God, no," I said. "I was through the war. Not over here, but in Europe."

"Europe?"

"North Africa and Italy. Is that important?"

"Very." Pock Marks wiped his mouth again. Then, confidentially, "Go to El Cairo tonight, anytime after nine. Agna is the singer there with the band. Tell her Goyo sent you. And bring your papers."

"Is that all you can tell me?" I asked.

He finished his beer and looked at me sadly.

"That's all for five pesos," he said. "Times being what they are." He turned quickly and disappeared out of the door.

I finished my beer and sat mulling over what Goyo had said. For five pesos he hadn't said much. Or had he? Whatever it was, none of it made sense. How could a seemingly harmless little ring—?

I started to take it out of my pocket again to look at it. Then I remembered Goyo's words: "you never know who may be watching." I pulled out my hand suddenly as if my pocket were hot. But whatever it was, I would have to go to El Cairo tonight. Apparently it was a nightclub, one that had been built since my time.

I glanced at my watch. It was after four. I suddenly realized how sticky I was, and that I wanted to go back to Candy's house for a shower.

Outside, I hailed the first vehicle that came my way, an ancient carromata pulled by a more ancient horse. It was fun to be on one again, bobbing up and down over the cobblestoned street. As we rumbled across the bridge, a breeze from the Pasig River dried my clothes and cooled my cheeks. I was beginning to feel at home again, and even though part of the city's beauty belongs to the past, Manila was, and always will be, my girl.

Now I was bursting with excitement. I wanted to tell Candy about my eventful afternoon. When I reached her house, I was disappointed to find that she was still out. I dashed upstairs, discarded my clothes and stepped into the shower. Then one of these things occurred that are always happening in the Orient. I turned on the tap but there was no water. I fiddled with the tap for a few minutes without any luck. I threw my robe around me and went out to the balcony.

"Oh, Lening," I called the maid. "What happened to the water?"

She stuck her head out of the kitchen door.

"Oh, sir, I am sorry," she said. "We will bring it up at once."

The two maids struggled upstairs with buckets of water and an empty wooden washtub.

"What happened to the faucet?" I asked.

"Since the war," Lening said, "we have water from it three days a week. All over the city it is that way. This is our night without electric light, too. If you do not like this way of bathing, the water may run a little in the shower later. After midnight."

"I'll take this, thanks," I laughed. "It's a long time till midnight."

When they were gone, I used one of the empty buckets to scoop water over my head and body. It was not quite as good as a real shower, but I felt refreshed. Afterwards I wrapped a towel around my body and threw myself across the wide low bed. The electric fan would not work, but there was a warm breeze blowing in from Manila Bay. I fell asleep.

Sometime later I was awakened by a series of sharp raps on the door.

"Gar, Gar!" I heard Candy's voice. "Are you awake?"

I sat up. It was dark. I stumbled around the room and found a match. In its flickering gleam, I saw a candle on the dresser. I lighted it.

"Are you dead or alive?" called Candy.

"Dead," I shouted through the door.

"Get some clothes on. Dinner is ready," said Candy. "I want to hear all about this afternoon."

"I have plenty to tell you," I said, struggling into fresh clothes. I found another candle stuck into a hurricane lamp. I finished dressing and slicked on my hair and appraised myself in the mirror.

"No wonder Grandmother thought Granddad was so handsome," I said loud. "By candlelight I'm not so bad myself."

"Are you talking to me or to yourself?" called Candy.

I opened the door.

"Are you still here?" I asked. "That's the kind of devotion I like. How do I look in candlelight?"

Candy sighed. "Don Juan," she said.

I rapped my chest.

"Grr. I'm a wolf by night. But it's the daylight that gets them."

"It's the night that gets me," laughed Candy.

I took her arm and we went downstairs.

"I thought you were going to meet us at the Manila Hotel bar," said Candy, handing me a pre-dinner martini.

"Sorry, I forgot all about it. Too many things were happening." Over a second drink I told her about the events of the afternoon.

"I don't understand it," she said. "I don't understand it at all. What do you suppose it means?"

"That's what I hope to find out tonight," I said. "At El Cairo."

"Oh, I'm glad we're going to El Cairo," she said.

I winked at the little red eye of the stuffed olive in my glass. The little red eye seemed to wink back.

"I'm going to El Cairo," I corrected her. "I'm sorry, Candy but it might not work if we showed up together. I have to see a girl. She might not talk if there were two of us."

She was disappointed, so throughout dinner I tried to keep up a flow of light banter. But I could see that she was absentminded. Finally she said, "Do you suppose some bandits are holding Clem for ransom?"

"Oh, that's too farfetched. But maybe the truth is even more fantastic." I laid my fork down. "From what I saw and heard this afternoon, I have a feeling there is some vicious organization at work. Some underground group."

"An organization for what?" asked Candy. "The war is over."

I shrugged. "I don't know all the answers. I've been back only one day. But there is something sinister in the air, and lots of little people are frightened."

She was suddenly quiet, as if she were trying to puzzle it all out, so I let the subject drop. After dinner we sat in the sala and talked and drank by candlelight until it was time for me to go. She gave me the keys to her car.

"It's only a jeep," she smiled. "Until times get better."

Suddenly she put her hands on my shoulders and pressed her lips against mine. "Be careful, Gar," said Candy.

I grabbed her.

"That's no way to make me careful," I said. I kissed her hard and left. I felt as if I could take apart any thug or conspirator who would stand in my way.

But the El Cairo proved what a poor prophet I was that night.

# FOUR

Downtown Manila on a night without electricity was a weird spectacle resembling a Halloween party. When I drove down Quezon Boulevard, all the small shops and restaurants glowed with red and yellow lights from candles and coconut-oil lamps. The pedestrians on the streets cast shadows like hobgoblins. Few people walk the streets of Manila at night. If you are well dressed you are apt to be banged over the head for your shoes and watch. If you are not well dressed, you are apt to be banged over the head anyway.

I was sorry when I left Quezon. It was one of the few paved streets in the city. But I swung to España to get to El Cairo. The street was a series of mountains and sudden valleys, unexpected boulders and memories of motor lorries. I could see now why the jeep was the most popular vehicle in the Philippines. No modern American motor car could have gone ten yards without breaking an axle.

The jeep rumbled up and down España into the quiet suburbs. Then I saw the flashing sign of EL CAIRO. No electrical shortage here. The jeep navigated the treacherous forty-five degree lane to the parking lot of the nightclub. I jumped out. Even after I turned off the motor the jeep kept rumbling like an eager bay hound, ready for the hunt. I patted its panting radiator.

"I wish I were a girl," I told Jeep. "You've got the body of a he-man and the heart of a tank."

A car attendant interrupted my romantic tryst. I straightened my tie, smoothed down my hair and went towards the bright lights.

The interior was an enormous room, gently lighted and adorned with many windows, so that it seemed like an open-air café. It was a favorite rendezvous of expatriate Americans, who, as the night wore on, became sentimental over expatriation, and of Manila socialites who became sentimental over sentiment. A middle-aged American was leading the orchestra with a tearful rendition of "Doodle-Dee-Doo." The other Americans joined the chorus lustily and the Manilans followed with a few shrill quavers. It was too young in the night for tears. The middle-aged American, I later learned, was the owner of the place, and the song was played at least three times every night.

I secured a table near the orchestra with the help of a five-peso bill, and ordered a drink. I asked the waiter when the floor show would go on.

"You are just in time, sir," he told me.

The lights dimmed and the orchestra leader took the mike. The first part of the show was a girl wearing red feathers and a red feather headdress; feathers on her hips, trailing down her legs like a tail; and a sequined bra. She did a mild imitation of a Folies Bergère dancer. Her partner was a young man in an evening suit who seemed bewildered, but he managed to catch her at the proper moments. Then came the singer, Agna. She was a thin, starved-looking creature, with overlarge eyes and overthin arms. Her voice rose huskily out of a cavern of feeling. She sang with the soul of a Fanny Brice.

I bought a small bright orchid from the flower girl and sent it to Agna through the waiter, inviting her to join me for a drink. The waiter returned and bowed like a High Chamberlain.

"Miss Agna sends her thanks for the flower, but she regrets she does not drink with the customers."

I was beginning to catch on.

"Tell her," I said, "that I am a friend of Goyo." I slipped the waiter another five pesos.

He bowed again and disappeared. In a few minutes Agna appeared. She came directly to my table, smiling brightly.

"Good evening," she said in a sweet high-pitched voice, "I haven't seen you for a long time."

"I couldn't remain away indefinitely," I said. "I like your singing." She smiled and sat down. I ordered drinks.

"I have been singing for a long time," she said. I studied her face. She was young but the freshness of youth was not in her face and her eyes told me she had indeed been singing for many people for a long time. A slum child who had grown up in the war, a child who knew all there was to know about people except that some people were nice.

"And how is my little friend Goyo?" asked Agna, sipping her drink.

"He sent me to you for help. I am looking for a friend."

Her eyes roved about the room carelessly.

"What sort of friend?" she asked.

"An American who fought the enemy."

"Do you know who is the enemy?" she asked in a bitter tone.

I tried to stand on neutral ground.

"We have the same enemy?" I said cautiously.

She pulled a cigarette from my pack and, putting it in her mouth, she thrust her face close to mine.

She said, "Do we? Do we have the same enemy? For people like you it doesn't really matter who wins. You are safe and secure. But for little people like us—." She puffed on the cigarette for a minute. "You do not know what the war was like for us. Our enemy was not the invader only. It was ourselves. We were in two camps. Oh, do not be fooled by what people tell you. Everybody says he was a guerilla. It is not so. There were the women who served the enemy, who entertained and slept with them in order to pass on information to their brothers hiding in the jungles. There were also the men and women who served and slept for money and clothes and special privileges. They were the enemy then, and they are still the enemy."

"My friend was one of the jungle brothers," I said.

Suddenly she smiled and touched my arm.

"This is a rhumba," she said. "Let us dance."

We moved around the floor to the strains of "Besame Mucho." Agna smiled again.

"Do you know that we are being watched?" she whispered.

My head involuntarily jerked around.

"Don't be a fool," said Agna. "Keep on dancing and I will show you the man."

We stood swaying close together. Then she pulled a compact out of her bosom and opened it, turning the mirror towards me. At first I could see only the reflections of the dancers, then a table next to mine appeared. There was a group of young men at the table. One of them was Pepe Gonzales.

"Do you know him?" asked Agna.

"I met him today," I said. "His name is Pepe Gonzales."

"Of the rich family?"

"The same."

The music stopped. She took my hand.

"I cannot talk to you any longer," she said. "Come to my room tonight. I leave here at two. The parking attendant will give you my address."

She smiled again and we shook hands. Then she left and disappeared behind the door beside the stage.

I called for my bill, paid it, and left. When I went out, I noticed Pepe was dancing.

I walked to the parking lot and gave the attendant the number of the jeep. He drove the car up to me and got out. I gave him a liberal tip.

"You have a message for me?" I said.

"What kind of message?" he asked.

"Agna the singer said you were to give me her address."

"Oh yes," he said. "You are the American she wishes to speak to. If you will come with me, she will speak to you herself."

I followed him. We walked across the parking lot to the back of the club. It was dark. I stumbled over a root and went down on my knee. As I went down, something that felt like an ax struck the back of my head and the lights went out.

It must have been a long time later. I seemed to hear distant voices. There was a terrific pain in my head. A little yellow light flickered in front of me and I smelled something sickening.

Then I discovered that I was awake and that my eyes were open. The little yellow light was the flame of a coconut-oil lamp and the smell came from burning oil. I blinked and tried to raise my head, but waves of nausea swept over me. I put my head down. Wherever I was laying, it was awfully hard. It reminded me of a foxhole in North Africa, only not as comfortable. I tried to raise my head again. I made it this time. I even got my shoulders up and leaned on my elbow. Now I understood why everything felt so hard. I was on the floor.

I was on the floor of an incredibly dingy little room. The coconut-oil lamp was on the floor and threw bobbing shadows on the walls. I was in a nipa house with a tin roof. The floor was split bamboo rails. I could hear chickens squawking and a pig grunting under the house. I wondered for a minute if I was out in the country.

There was a movement on my left. I turned my head without thinking. Shafts of pain darted in my eyes. Then I saw the red glow of a cigarette, then a thin brown hand, then a small woman's body. Agna was looking down at me.

"Well," I said bitterly, "that parking attendant certainly gave me the right address."

"I do not know what you mean," said Agna. "When I came home I found you lying in front of my house. I brought you in so you would not be run over."

I looked at my suit. Sure enough, I had been lying some place. The front of my coat and trousers were caked with dried mud. My face felt stiff with the stuff, too.

"Now that I'm here," I said, "what shall we talk about?"

"I do not know you," said Agna. "I do not want to know you. Now, please go."

I scrambled to my feet and grabbed her arm.

"I came here to talk and we're going to talk," I said.

"I don't know anything you want to know," she said, pulling away from me. "Now get out of here or I will have to call my friends."

"Both of them," said a voice behind me.

I turned around. In the shadows at the far end of the room was an opening into another room. In the opening stood two figures. Both wore dark suits. Both wore hats that threw their faces in shadow. The taller man had a gun pointed at me.

"Get out," said Agna. "Your jeep is outside. Go back where you came from."

Her turn-about attitude maddened me. I had been back in Manila less than twenty-four hours. I had been on one goose chase after another. I had been beat over the head, and here, when I was on the verge of learning what I wanted, I was being dismissed by a sultry female.

I pulled open my wallet. It was my only chance.

"I came to tell you, Agna," I said, "that I haven't got all of that thousand pesos on me. But I'll get it for you tomorrow. Thanks for your information. Here's a fifty on account."

I threw the money on a table and went outside. I found my jeep across the street. I looked around at the dark squares of nipa houses and barong-barongs and realized I was in Tondo, the slum district.

I got in the jeep and drove away. At the first corner I turned, drove to the end of the street, and parked in the shadow of a shack. Then I got out and walked between clusters of silent shacks to a spot where I could see Agna's house.

Then while I stood there a faint weird sound broke through the silent darkness. I strained my ears, trying to identify it. Suddenly it seemed as if I were back in the mountains of Baguio and the Igorots were playing on their reed flutes. There is no music like it in the world. I stood wondering if one of the mountain men had come down into the city. The music stopped abruptly and the night was as deadly still as before.

While I waited in the shadow of a tree, I saw the two men come out of Agna's place and walk down the dark road. One of them carried a flashlight. I could see the beam cutting the darkness. Then a car door slammed. A motor roared, and they were gone.

I ran across the road. I climbed the bamboo ladder and pushed the door open. I saw Agna sprawled across the mat. She looked asleep. Her cigarette was still burning on the mat. I stepped on it. I bent over Agna. Then I saw she wasn't sleeping. There was a dark spot on her white dress. The spot was widening. I touched the spot. It was warm and wet. She was stabbed near the heart.

I got some water from a clay pitcher and washed her face. I tried to stop the flow of blood with my handkerchief. She opened her eyes and looked at me.

"You—shouldn't—have said that," she whispered. "About—the—money."

"I'm sorry," I said humbly. "I didn't know they would do this to you."

"They are—in the pay of—both sides," she said. "There is a great conspiracy in Manila. They came—to warn me—not to talk to you. I was being—watched." She puffed on the cigarette I held to her lips and sighed. "It's funny," she smiled. "I lived through the war—but I—can't live through—the peace." She closed her eyes, but suddenly they were open again. In the dim light, her eyes had the lonely look of a young child who has heard of Christmas but never saw it. "To—find your friend," she whispered, then stopped. Her breath was coming in gasps. "Go back where you came from."

I put my ear close to her lips. But her head rolled down my arms. Then she was still. I laid her down gently.

Suddenly, I heard the rustle of air. The door opened slowly. I jumped and grabbed a pair of legs. He went down with me. He struck at my face. I threw myself on top of him and beat his head against the floor. He was a little fellow. But he could kick. We rolled over and over and slid out the door and fell down to the ground. Then someone else jumped on my back, and I saw the quick flash of a knife.

Suddenly a voice said, "Look out! The police!"

The big fellow and the little one knocked me over as they scrambled to their feet. Then they ran into the darkness. I started to chase them, but somebody grabbed my arm. I looked around. There stood Pepe.

"Let them go," he said. "That's the best way to get rid of anybody around here. All you have to do is yell 'The police are here!' and everybody disappears."

"What are you doing here?" I asked.

"I've been playing merry-go-round with you all evening. I followed you when you left El Cairo. I intended to ask you to join my table. When I saw those two bash you over the head and drive off, I decided you had found more fun than I. My party was dull anyway, so I followed you. Fine choice of friends you've got here in Tondo… What happened inside?"

"They killed Agna."

Pepe was silent a minute. Then he said, "Did you leave any evidence of having been there?"

"I suppose so," I said. "Cigarette butts and my handkerchief. And I handled the water pitcher."

"You wait here," said Pepe. "No need for you to get mixed up in a police investigation."

I leaned against the house, trying to get my bearings. In a few minutes Pepe came out. We walked back to my jeep.

"I'll call the police when I get home," said Pepe.

I started the motor and we drove off in a series of jerks over the rough lane. The pain in my head was coming back and my mind was whirling crazily. But one thing stood out: Pepe's timely appearance was just a little too pat.

I wondered if he had any connection with Agna's death.

# FIVE

Every time I dozed off that night, all I could see was Agna's face and the widening pool of blood on her dress, and I was torn with a feeling of guilt.

I rolled and tossed around painfully. I hadn't been in a physical scrap[e] since the war and many unused muscles and strained tendons cried out every time I moved. I took a couple of aspirins to stop the pain in my head, but my mind was so keyed up that sleep was impossible.

I finally gave up, opened a bottle of rye and sat drinking and smoking until dawn brought into view the broken hulks of sunken ships in Manila Bay.

I had a good view of the street to the beach. In the clear thin light of early morning, the trees and bushes emerged from the shadows. The birds were beginning to stir. I caught the fragrance of gardenias and ripe mangoes.

I got up and put on my swimming trunks. I left the house and walked to the beach. The air was as clean and sweet as the breath of a young girl. At the water's edge, I stopped and looked down the boulevard to the Manila Hotel, then out to the shadowy rock of Corregidor. For a while, the morning and I shared a warm secret: we possessed Manila at her best.

Finally I slipped into the water and paddled around, keeping an eye for bloodsucking jellyfish. The pains in my joints slowly disappeared. My head began to feel light.

I came out of the water and sat on the sand. I found myself reviewing the events of the past night. Taken individually, they didn't make sense, but collectively they revealed a kind of pattern.

An underworld or an underground of unimportant little people were allied against another group of whom they were in mortal terror. That much I could gather from Agna and her conversation and the swiftness with which the two thugs had dispatched her. The information she had given me was so generalized that it was tough to draw definite conclusions.

She had said, "To find your friend, go back where you came from." What in Sam Hill did she mean?

I went back to the water absorbed in thought. I was frowning and treading water as I thought over her words and did not see the big roller until it dashed upon me. The wave hit me with a bang, threw me into a somersault and carried me high up on the beach.

"Whew!" I said aloud. "That certainly brought me back where I came from!"

And with that, light broke in my mind. Agna's remark could only mean one thing. Back where I came from must mean the trinket shop where I had started the hunt.

I was through swimming for the day. I wrapped the robe around me and trotted back to the house. It did not take me long to dress. I intended to be at the shop before it opened. I slipped my service gun in my hip.

When I was going out I heard someone stirring in the kitchen. I stuck my head in the door. Lening was bringing water from the well outside.

"When Mrs. Mayo comes down, tell her I had to go out early," I said. "I'll be back when I get here."

"Would you not care for breakfast, sir?" asked Lening.

"No thanks," I said. "I'll eat out."

I walked lightly down the street. I glanced at my watch. It was only six o'clock. This was like being back in the Army. I passed the Army and Navy Club and, further on, a couple of pre-war pretentious apartment houses that had been only partly damaged and were being rapidly glued together again to relieve the housing shortage.

People began to appear in the streets, cars began to fill the stream of traffic; horns were honking, dogs and cats and a few pigs came out of hiding. Manila was awake! Life starts early over here. At the crack of dawn the streets fill up. After sunset they are empty. With the night comes the terror that has never left the city since the war days.

I reached the ruins of the government buildings and the junction of three bridges that crossed the river to the city proper. I stopped for a minute in the middle of the bridge to watch a small craft being unloaded. The workmen paused to wave at me. I grinned and waved my hat. Friendly people, these people over here. Their salute reminded me that for some of them trouble was not yet over and that somehow Clem was mixed up in the mysterious tangle and, finally, that I was hungry enough to eat a carabao.

I crossed the bridge and entered the Escolta, and stopped at the first eating place. I had my favorite breakfast from the old days: mangoes and papaya and rice cakes, washed down with half a gallon of iced coffee.

By this time it was nearly eight o'clock. I walked down the Escolta to the end of the street. Here I paused and looked around. Then I saw something I had not noticed yesterday.

A dark narrow alley cut this side of the Escolta from the street at the corner. It was not much wider than the width of a big man. It looked like one of those narrow alleys in a Chinese quarter.

I stepped into the alley. It was littered with trash and bits of fallen plaster. It reeked with an awful smell of decaying garbage and excrement. I held my handkerchief to my nose and tried to breathe through my mouth. I walked on. I saw the back of the trinket shop with its barred window. I approached it and peered inside. All I could see were shelves stocked with goods, boxes on the floor, and a big desk.

I walked around to the front of the shop, ducking under the same long line of dripping wash. The family across the street was squatting in the doorway. I peered inside the window of the shop. No one was around. That was strange. Most of the shops were beginning to open. Then I saw a hole where the keyhole should have been. I tried the door. It was held securely by an inside bolt. That meant someone was inside. Perhaps the family lived upstairs.

I knocked heavily on the door. For a long time there was no answer. Then, from above, a window was pushed open.

"Go away," said a woman's voice.

I looked up. A middle-aged Filipina leaned out of the upper window. Her black hair was streaming over her shoulder; her face was flushed with weeping.

"I want to see your husband," I told her.

An outburst of weeping shook her. Her plump shoulders heaved convulsively.

"Go away, go away!" she cried.

"Are you in trouble?" I asked. "Can I help you?"

"My husband is dead," sobbed the woman.

"Please let me in," I said. "I am a friend."

Another face appeared at the window. It was the young salesgirl. Her hair was drawn back into a tight little knot now. She wore no gay lip rouge this morning. She looked pinched. She began to talk excitedly in Tagalog.

"That's the man! That's the man who frightened Papa yesterday. He is not our friend!"

I answered her back in Tagalog. "I did not mean to frighten your father. I only wanted to talk to him. I'm sorry he is dead. When did he die?"

"He died this morning," said the woman. "Someone broke in and stabbed him."

"Maybe you did it," said the girl harshly. "Now, go away or we will call the police."

They withdrew from the window and closed it. I leaned against the wall and lit a cigarette. My hands were shaking.

Two deaths in twelve hours, because of me. Needless deaths, even from the other gang's point of view. Nobody had told me anything. I had not learned a single word that was useful to me in my search for Clem. Yet two people who knew something were now dead because they had talked with me.

Two deaths from stabbing. A knife is a silent weapon. It gives no warning and elicits no shout. Agna had been expertly stabbed near the heart. I had no doubt the poor little shopkeeper had received it the same way. The man who uses a knife is a peculiar type of killer. An American cannot use a knife effectively. The knife killer must know how to creep up on his victim, pounce and insert the blade with just the right amount of strength. It is the weapon of oppressed men, men who have had their

34

education in the dark alleys and fought with their backs to the wall.

I wasn't looking for the killer. For even if I caught him and turned him over to the police, others would take his place. These were thugs in the pay of someone, some individual or group of individuals, so ruthless that human life meant nothing. Whoever they were, they had a terrific stake. They were desperate.

I started down the street, away from Escolta. I walked to the dock and stood looking at the moving water of the Pasig River.

I was at a dead end. I had nothing to go on but Agna's advice. I went over our meeting, from the time she came to my table until we parted. She had kept talking about some enemy— the enemy who had served the invaders during the war.

I didn't have information yet to do me any good, but if what I believed was true, there was a diabolical conspiracy in Manila.

I had to talk to somebody, somebody who could give me a definite lead. Somewhere in this surrealist picture Clem and his ring fitted in. Who could help me? Pepe Gonzales? I shook my head. Pepe was only a playboy, and it was quite probable that he was on the other side of the fence.

It was while I stood there leaning against a post the answer came walking towards me.

Goyo.

He hadn't seen me yet. I averted my face until he was almost beside me. Then I swung around.

"Goyo!" I said.

His brown face blanched and the pockmarks stood out like craters on his chin. He swung on his heels and scurried away like a rabbit. I ran after him. He was small, but he was light on his feet. He sailed along like a feather, dodging in and out among the pedestrians.

I almost lost him at the corner. I was delayed by a man with a big paunch. When I turned the corner, Goyo was halfway down the block. He did not look back once. He kept running.

Then I got a break. He was stopped at the crossing by a crowd of pedestrians. He leaped into the middle of the street, but just then one of the inevitable horse-drawn carromatas appeared and stopped him. I had finally caught up with him. I grabbed his arms. He pulled away so fast that he almost lost his coat. But I held on to him as if he were a pot of gold.

I shouted to the carromata driver to stop. I hoisted Goyo aboard. I told the driver Candy's address. The whip cracked and the small horse broke into a run.

I looked at Goyo. He was shrunk back into the other corner of the seat. His knees were shaking and his teeth were chattering. I began to realize how Frankenstein must have felt when everybody shrieked and ran away from him. I pushed a cigarette into Goyo's mouth and lit it for him.

"Take it easy," I told him. "You're going home with me where you'll be safe. You can have all the beer with whisky chasers you want and I'll give you money. I only want to talk."

He kept shaking his head and moaning. I was glad when we reached the house. Candy herself opened the door. She looked bewildered when she saw Goyo.

"This is a friend of mine," I said. "I'm going to take him to my room. Send up some breakfast and some beer, will you?"

Candy grasped the situation at once. She nodded and went into the kitchen. I dragged Goyo upstairs. I pushed him inside the room. He fell across the bed and started moaning again.

I gave him a stiff slug of rye. Then he stopped shaking and some color came to his face. He sat silently on the edge of the bed, fingering his pockmarks until Lening arrived with a tray.

I never saw a man eat so fast in my life. He went after the food like a hungry dog, chewing great hunks of fried ham and pushing whole fried eggs into his mouth. He even chewed the mango skin. I poured him a beer. He drank the beer in one gulp. Then he looked up at me and grinned.

Nothing about this whole business touched me as much as Goyo's grin. Feed a hungry pup and he's your pal. Feed a poor guy that's starved most of his life and—I began to understand a lot of things about people I had not thought much of before. Now I understood why everything in Manila had to be prefaced with five pesos.

"Feeling better?" I asked Goyo.

He nodded. I sat down on the edge of the bed beside him. I offered him a cigarette.

"Goyo," I said slowly, trying to choose my words as if I were talking to a child, "I am your friend. I was Agna's friend. I am the friend of all people like you who suffered during the war. I want to help you. Will you tell me what you know about all this business?"

He glanced around the room nervously.

"Nobody can hear us," I told him. "The people in this house are your friends."

"There is not much I can tell you," he said finally. "During the war some of us fought the enemy through the underground. We cheated them, we lied to them, we stole from them whatever we could. We passed information to each other. Some of us were caught and sent to Fort Santiago. Some of us died there. Some of us came out crippled. Those of us who came out never forgot."

"Go on," I said.

He took a deep breath. Then he continued. "There were many among our people who played with the enemy. They did not lose their homes. They built bigger homes and bought cars. They were not tortured. They were the ones who told on us."

I poured him another drink.

"The war is over now," he went on, "and the people who played with the enemy want us to forget what they did. They try to pretend they were with us but we know differently. Now they are afraid of being arrested and tried by the War Crimes Court. So they have organized themselves. They punish anyone who speaks against them. We are all afraid."

"What about this ring?" I asked, taking Clem's ring out of the dresser drawer.

"During the war," said Goyo, "I saw that ring. Whenever it appeared in Manila it meant a message of some kind. I do not know what the message was. The ring was passed among us from one to the other until it reached a certain man. He knew what it meant. But we were always happy when we saw the ring. We knew it came from a group of guerillas and that they were planning something."

"Isn't there anyone who can tell me about the ring—where it comes from and what it means?" I asked.

Goyo hesitated. His nervous eyes darted around the room again. He leaned close to me.

"The man with the earring can tell you."

"Where can I find him?"

Goyo shrugged.

"I do not know. But somewhere among your friends, among people you know, you will find the man with the earring. He has not stopped working." He looked at me plaintively. "That's all I know."

I pressed a roll of notes in his hand.

"Thanks, Goyo. If you ever need help, come to me. My name is Gar Stanley and I am your friend."

He grinned and eyed the bottle again. I gave him another drink. "Would you like to stay here until it's dark?" I asked.

He put down the empty glass and shook his head.

"I get along all right," he said. "I've lived here all my life. No one will ever catch Goyo as long as there is a dark alley."

He opened the door and grinned at me. Then he went out. He was a gallant little guy.

When the door closed behind him, a great weariness hit me and I realized I had not slept all night. I flopped across the bed and was asleep before I found the pillow.

# SIX

For the next few days I felt like a fellow who has bought one Christmas present too many. The information Goyo had given me was like a package that I didn't know who to give to, or how. Candy and I talked the situation over. She racked her brains but could not recall having seen among her friends a man with an earring.

"Only the Igorots in Baguio wear earrings," said Candy, "and they very rarely come to Manila. Besides, I wouldn't know anyone among them."

The word Igorot teased at my memory. It seemed that there was something connected with the Igorots in this affair that I should remember. But, try as I would, I could not recall what the association was.

"I have a hunch," I said, "that the key to this whole thing is somewhere in the mountains. This ring was made there and the man I want to see is evidently one of the mountain people."

"Why don't we go up there?" she asked.

I shook my head.

"Even if I went there now nobody would talk to me unless I was sent by one of their own men. A man could hide for a lifetime in those mountains and one could not find him unless he wanted to be found."

"Do you suppose Pepe could help us?"

"I'm afraid to trust him," I said. "The way he popped up that night when Agna was killed leads me to believe he may be mixed up in this somewhere. And if he is, he's on the other side. He and his family are the kind who would have too much to lose.

I think our best bet is to start circulating among our friends, keeping our eyes open and our ideas to ourselves."

"Good," said Candy. "Then we can begin by playing bridge with the Millers tonight. He is a building contractor."

"Bridge!" I said. "I said circulating, not shuffling."

"We have to start somewhere," said Candy. "It will be good for you. It has a civilizing effect."

"If I wanted to be civilized, I would never have come back to Manila," I told her. "I'd have stayed in Frisco where people act civilized by getting drunk twice a day and bedding blondes they pick up in bars."

"Gar!" said Candy. "The war certainly changed you."

I reached over and pulled her close to me.

"I'm a big boy now, Mama," I told her.

There is no telling where this interesting conversation would have led us had not Lening suddenly appeared at the door of the patio and announced that Mr. Gonzales was waiting in the sala.

"Oh, bother," muttered Candy, slipping out of my half nelson. "He's getting to be a prize nuisance."

But she managed to sweeten her face when Pepe came into view, immaculate as ever in tropical whites.

"I am glad to find you both here," said Pepe. "I have a message for you from my sister in Quezon City. She is giving an impromptu dinner and wants you both to come."

"We're very—" began Candy.

But I interrupted her, "Is your sister a bridge fiend?"

"Well—ah—don't you like badminton and moonlight bathing?" asked Pepe.

"We love it!" I said. "Nothing could keep us away."

Candy glared at me from behind Pepe's shoulder, but there was nothing she could say. When Pepe was gone, she started cussing me.

"You men are all alike, always thinking of yourselves," she complained.

"Look," I told her, "if you don't want to go, just send word that you've come down with an attack of leprosy. For myself, I think it's important. We'll never learn anything from newcomers to Manila like the Millers, or from any other Americans, for that matter. It's not because Americans are so pure and holy that they wouldn't bargain for favors when they were up against it, but ninety-nine percent of them were locked up during the war. The answer to this lies with the people who were roaming loose at that time—the Spanish nationals, the Filipinos, the mestizos, and even the Chinese."

"What an international social life we're going to have!" declared Candy. Then she quieted down. "I guess you're right, Gar," she said. "I can put up with it for Clem's sake."

When it comes to a party, no one can throw one with more flavor than a rich Manilan. Pepe's sister, Elena, was no exception. She was a small-bosomed girl with the great expressive eyes and soft lips of an El Greco Virgin. Her husband, Tomas Hernandez, was short and inclined to be hippy, with a cuddly waistline and disarming smile. He was, Pepe told me, a successful attorney whose teeth were well sunk into the political bone. But it must have been a very soft bone.

Their home was an imitation of a Hollywood movie producer's, complete with air conditioning. The party itself belonged strictly to affluent Manila people. The women were as exotic as ginger flowers, dressed with expensive simplicity, coiffured to the hilt with upswept hairdos of intricate coils and curls, and smelling to high heaven of Chanel No. 5. The men were inclined to group among themselves and grow red in the face after two light drinks, while their wives demurely sipped Sunday School punch or pure fruit juice.

It takes a party of this kind quite a while to get under way. It took exactly twenty minutes in this case. Pepe deftly slipped a couple of quarts of gin in the punch bowl, and after that everybody became giggly and friendly-eyed.

I found myself surrounded by a girl with eyes like wild plums, wearing a white orchid over each ear, who confided to me breathlessly that her name was Estara Montalvo; that her father owned an automobile and two banks, or maybe it was the other way around (I had some of the punch, too); and that American men thrilled her.

I sat back and looked at her again. After all, an automobile and two banks, or even one bank, is not something to be passed over lightly. She was the typical ginger-flower type, with the heart-shaped face and elongated eyes that started such songs as "When I Go Back to Samoa I'll Leave No Moah."

"Are you married?" I asked.

She giggled.

"Not yet," she said. "I've turned down ever so many offers, but I'm waiting for the right man."

"What's the right man like?" I asked.

My words sent a positive tremor through her.

"Oh," said Estara, "he must be strong and intelligent and —and strong—and sweep me away as if he were carrying me off on a white horse."

"You wouldn't settle for a fellow with just a jeep that isn't his, would you?" I asked.

She edged a little closer.

"Oh, that would be all right," she said. "My father has—"

"I know. An automobile and two banks."

She tittered again.

"You've got it backwards."

"I've got the idea, though," I told her.

Our tender rhapsody was broken up when dinner was announced. I found myself back in Candy's hands.

"I trust," said Candy, "that I haven't broken up the Great Love of the twentieth century."

"You have," I told her. "I was just about to inherit an automobile and two banks with a ginger-flower thrown in."

Candy looked at me carefully.

"You've been drinking, " she told me, without tenderness.

"Drink," I said, "has such civilizing effect. Don't you agree?"

That settled Candy. It settled her so much that she didn't talk to me for the rest of dinner.

Since Candy chose to ignore me and since the woman on my left was a bucktoothed matron whose conversational ability was limited to much head nodding and vigorous affirmatives to everything I said, I had plenty of chance to study the other guests.

In the old days, because of my father's business, we had mingled as much with the wealthy native residents as we did with Americans. But to my surprise, there was not a single person at the table whose family name recalled any of my old friends. It was surprising because, in a place like Manila, families stay put for generations. These people may have been old Manila hands, but I had never heard of any of them before I went away. Ordinarily the system of things doesn't change that fast in the tropics, but here it was obvious that the Ins were out and that the former Outs had moved up into the inner circle of money and social position. Only the war could have accomplished this radical social change.

It would be an interesting thing, I thought, to learn just how many of these people could trace their present fortunes directly to shadowy deals made through the enemy during the war. Oh, don't mistake me. These people were not vulgarians like our ideas of the newly rich. They knew which forks to use and how to make polite small talk. But there was something lacking in them. They had a certain nervous tension under the cover of laughter and efforts at gaiety. That was it. They were all working too hard at it. I caught some of them eyeing me from time to time.

I began to wonder if I was the reason for the impromptu party. It was just a little too carefully staged to be one of those things that grow out of a hostess' last-minute whim. If the show was for my benefit, it meant that my trail was getting hot and that some people were frightened. If that was so, somebody should approach me before the evening was over.

I decided to sit back and take it easy on the liquor. When dinner was over we all moved out to the terrace for coffee and brandy.

But as the evening wore on there was not a single person who seemed to linger in my company longer than anyone else. For a while I sat with my host, Hernandez, and a couple of others—a fellow named Estacio who was the owner of a new daily newspaper and somebody named Ramirez who was opening a broadcasting station, two enterprises which would take plenty of capital.

Then a band started up. The drinking and dancing went on simultaneously, and I was passed around like a loving cup from one glamour girl to another. But it seemed that no matter who I started out with, I always ended up with Estara. She was becoming a menace. I know these tropical gals. They will only give you the glad-eye to a certain point, then when you start pawing around they giggle and run and expect you to present their fathers with an affidavit of your honorable intentions.

I wanted to shake her off so that I could spend more time with Estacio and Ramirez. They were two bright boys who might, under the influence of liquor, drop a word or two that would give me a lead. I tried soaking Estara in champagne, but I gave it up when I caught her pouring it out the window. It began to look as if the evening would be a total loss. Yet I had the feeling that this was all a big act and that somewhere there was a part in it for me.

After a while the dancing stopped and then something took place which is inevitable at every party in the Philippines. The hostess always has a dear friend who has studied opera. In this case it was my self-appointed girl friend, Estara.

After much giggling and encouragement she was propelled to the piano. Then, once having a firm clutch on the instrument, she seemed equally determined never to leave it, and we had to sit through shrill renditions from *Madame Butterfly*, the Bell Song from *Lakmé* and – God help us all – she even tried *The Cry of the Valkerie*.

She murdered one song after another. I writhed in agony. Finally, Candy took pity on me.

"Isn't this awful?" muttered Candy.

"Let's go outside and get drunk," I whispered.

We were edging towards the terrace when it happened. A piercing wail shook the whole house. We all stared at Estara in dumbfoundment. We hadn't thought her capable of that. Estara stopped in the middle of a trill and gaped back at us. Then the wail was repeated in a rising cadenza of hysteria. But by this time we realized that Estara was not to blame. The noise came from upstairs.

The men rushed for the stairs. One of the maids came running down.

"A burglar! A burglar!" she cried, pointing wildly upwards. "He gone out the window."

Some of the men ran outside. The others went upstairs. I stayed where I was. Later I wished I had taken part in the hunt outside. In a few minutes they caught the housebreaker and dragged him into the house.

I took one look at the shabby figure in black alpaca and groaned to myself. It was my friend Goyo.

Everybody was talking all at once and shouting questions at him. Goyo did not once look in my direction. He simply hung his head and refused to talk. A search of his body disclosed no loot. Evidently he had just broken into the house. Ramirez became quite bitter at Goyo's silence. He started to smack him around.

"Wait a minute," I intervened. "Let the police do that. Has anybody called them yet?"

Everybody remarked at my brilliance. It took three of them to call the police. They gagged and bound Goyo as if he were a prize prisoner of war and locked him in the liquor pantry while they awaited the arrival of the police. Probably the whole force would show up for this, I thought. I had visions of the agony Goyo was going through in the liquor pantry, eyeing all those bottles of bonded stuff and unable to get his hands on anything.

But Pepe's sister was a good hostess. To take her guests' minds off the excitement, she ordered the band to start up again. In a few minutes everybody was swinging around the room in a samba.

I told Candy to keep Pepe dancing so that he couldn't follow me. When I saw Estara heading my way, I ducked out the window and ran around to the back of the house.

The servants were all gathered in the kitchen, eating and talking their heads off about the attempted burglary. There was no chance of getting in through there unnoticed. I continued walking around the house. There was a small window between the kitchen and dining room. It was one of the few windows without bars, probably because it was high off the ground.

I hoisted myself up and peered inside. Goyo was sitting on a reed chair and gazing mournfully at the rows of bottles lining the shelves. Even with his mouth bound, the expression on his face was so filled with frustrated longing that I could not resist chuckling to myself.

I jumped down to the ground and let myself into the dining room through the french doors. I knew I had to hurry. The music had just stopped and people would spill all over the house again.

Nobody had bothered to remove the key from the lock

of the liquor closet. I quickly stepped inside. Goyo's eyes lighted up when he saw me. I guess he had figured he was really in for it this time. I cut him loose with my pocket knife.

"For God's sake," I said, "what made you try a mad stunt like housebreaking?"

"I am not a professional housebreaker," said Goyo with dignity, rubbing his sore mouth where the gag had cut his lips. "I am a pickpocket, and a very good one, too."

"You didn't expect to pick pockets here, did you?" I asked.

He eyed me solemnly. Then he said, "I came here to warn you. I heard about this party. It is a plan to trap you."

"Who laid the trap?" I asked.

Before Goyo could answer, we heard footsteps in the dining room. I opened the window. It was small, but big enough for a fellow his size.

"Get out of here," I whispered, "Get in touch with me at my house."

He was in a hurry, all right. But before he scrambled through the window he found time to grab one of the bottles off the shelf. He swung on the window sill and looked at me for a minute, shaking his head sadly. Then he dropped to the ground, into the darkness.

The footsteps in the dining room ceased. I figured that whoever it was had gone away, so I quietly opened the door. I found myself staring at Estara.

She peered over my shoulder at the empty room and opened window. Suddenly, she looked at me like a cat that has just made a killing.

"Now, why did you do a thing like that?" she asked.

I felt as guilty as a pickpocket caught red-handed. I fumbled for something to say.

Then I knew what Goyo had meant by a trap.

And I realized that I had fallen neatly into one.

# SEVEN

There was a commotion at the front door when the police arrived. A couple of uniformed men and all the guests came marching our way.

I'll say this for Estara. She was quick on the trigger. She ran towards the police, crying, "He escaped!"

"What?" shouted Estacio, pressing forward. He ran to the door of the little room and looked inside. He swung on me.

"How did this happen?" he demanded.

I shrugged.

"I haven't the faintest idea," I said.

Estara spoke up quickly.

"We came here together to see him, and he was gone."

By this time everybody was around the little door. The police went inside the room and examined the cut strips of cloth that had bound Goyo.

"Who tied him?" asked one of the policemen.

"I did," said Pepe. He was so close to me that I jumped. I looked at him. He was grinning ruefully. "I'm afraid I'm not much good at tying up people. He probably had no trouble slipping out of his bonds."

"These have been cut," said the other policeman.

Pepe shrugged. "He must have torn them apart on the corner of the chair."

Pepe's brother-in-law broke into the conversation.

"After all, there's no real harm done," Hernandez said. "The man did not take anything."

"It's the principle of it," declared Estacio, his face growing red. "Everybody complains that Manila is overrun with thugs

47

and footpads and when we catch one he gets away. I'm going to write an editorial about it!"

"Well, leave my name out of your editorial," said Hernandez. "Or every burglar in town will be out here."

The police went outside to search the grounds. Some of the men joined them. I knew, however, that by this time Goyo was far away. Thanks to Estara, nobody held me responsible. I even considered the possibility of making her believe what Pepe had suggested: that Goyo had freed himself.

"They should have tied him up with something stronger than cotton strips," I remarked as we walked towards the terrace. "Cotton is very easy to cut on a sharp edge."

"Do you suppose he was talking to himself while he cut his bonds?" she asked.

I tried to bluff it out.

"How should I know?" I asked. "He was gone when I looked inside."

"Of course," she smiled. But she was no fool. She knew I had freed Goyo and she knew that I knew. To prove her point she added casually, "Will you come and have merienda with us tomorrow? Mother would be delighted to hear of your war experiences."

What could I do? I knew when I was a cooked goose. However, I decided, Estara might not know it but she was going to lead me to what I wanted. If I started palling around with her, I knew I would eventually find the man with the earring.

In the Philippines, merienda is the equivalent of an afternoon tea. But instead of tea—nobody drinks the stuff here except those with "stoo-mock trr-oble"—thick spiced chocolate is served and chilled fruit and sweet cakes.

When I arrived at Estara's house, I found myself in the position of a character out of Gilbert & Sullivan. Papa Montalvo was missing—presumably, he was busy b.uying more banks—but I had to run through a whole reception line of her mother, brothers, sisters, and uncles.

Mama was a handsome matron with graying hair who looked like a middle-aged version of Olivia de Havilland. The younger women provided mostly background music. It was the men who had the flash. They were as handsome and talkative as tropical birds. Even Estara, who had been full of such bright tricks the night before, sat demurely between two of her sisters, with her hands folded. Whenever Mama spoke they all nodded in unison, like a silent chorus.

Mama Montalvo started the conversation by asking me about my part in the war, but before I had a chance to tell her, she rolled her big eyes, declaring how they had all suffered.

She looked around her with approval as her family bobbed their heads vigorously in confirmation.

"It was horrible!" said Mama, who looked as if nothing more horrible had ever happened to her than to run out of bicarbonate of soda.

"Was there much shortage of food?" I asked.

"We did not go hungry," answered one of the younger girls.

"She means we ate almost everyday," interposed Mama with a brave smile. "Fortunately for us, my husband was in a business that the enemy wanted him to continue operating."

"I should think the owner of a bank would have found it pretty rough," I commended. "The rate of exchange was falling pretty fast, wasn't it?"

"Oh, Papa didn't own the bank then," said the same younger sister.

I looked at her with interest. Here was a kid full of news. If I could only get her alone for fifteen minutes she could probably uncover more dirt than a private investigator. But Mama Montalvo was glaring at her and smiling at me at the same time—which, by the way, was quite a feat. They say you only learn the trick in finishing schools.

"The former bank president was an American who died in concentration," Mama explained. "My husband was forced to take over. Oh, it was terrible!" She sighed as she munched a piece of cake.

"They even forced us to sell them what we raised on our hacienda," said one of the uncles.

Evidently they were going to toss the talk around like a volleyball so that Little Sister could not spill any more state secrets.

"You have a hacienda?" I asked politely.

He nodded. "In Cebu. The enemy came down there and allotted us a small portion of the crop and forced us to sell them the rest."

"We had hardly enough to eat," said Mama, pouring another cup of chocolate.

"The worst of it was," said another uncle, "the peasants would come at night and steal chickens and rice and whatever else they could lay their hands on. We even had to post guards down there."

I'll bet you did, I thought. I'll bet you had to post guards with guns to shoot your neighbors who were starving because their crops were taken by the enemy and they weren't getting paid for it.

For a minute I had a hard time refraining myself from making verbal cracks about their patriotism. Instead I managed to say,

"The guerillas were pretty active, weren't they?"

"We were all guerillas," said one of the young man. "I was a captain."

"I was a colonel," said another.

"I was a major," said a third.

They all grinned at me in comradely fashion.

"You all outrank me," I said. "I went in a private. I came out the same way."

Everybody laughed. The tension that Youngster Sister had stirred up disappeared. Mama pushed a bowl of American apples towards me. Estara passed me some cookies with her own little hands. Uncle gave me a cigar. I had made the grade. I was considered one of them.

Nice people.

So for the next couple of weeks I gave a fair imitation of an ardent suitor. I sent Estara flowers and candy and invited the clan to dinner at the Manila Hotel. I had not as yet met Papa. He was, they told me, away on a trip. They had written him about me and he was eager to meet me.

They invited me on picnics and little dinner parties, and Estara began talking about a house party they were planning to give at the hacienda. In fact, I was seen so much in Estara's company that Pepe began to kid me.

"Now you're cooking, as you Americans say," he would say, clapping me on the back in a brotherly fashion.

I began to wonder, however, if I were really cooking or being roasted in slow fire. No matter how many places we went or how many people we saw—and we covered most of the upper set in Manila—I had not seen any sign of the man with the earring.

I had seen Goyo a few times. We had gotten into the habit of meeting at the little bar where he first talked to me. He had nothing to report, however, even though by this time I was practically supporting him.

Gradually it began to dawn on me that I was being taken in by the oldest methods. I was offered Estara in their ever polite way, and the chance to join their ranks, in exchange for my dropping my interest in Clem's disappearance. Pretty subtle, these people!

Worst of all, I was having Candy trouble.

Candy had been opposed to the whole deal from the time that I told her about it.

"It would have been better to let Goyo get caught than involve yourself the way you did," she said.

"How can you say a thing like that?" I asked. "You know what would have happened to him. They would have made an example of him and thrown him the book."

"All I know," said Candy, "is that none of this is helping you find Clem."

Something in her voice made me look at her sharply. I was shocked at how pinched and drawn her face had become. There were blue circles under her eyes, evidence of long sleepless nights. It dawned on me that she was worrying herself sick over this thing.

"Candy," I said, as gently as I could, "has it ever occurred to you that this ring might not be from Clem? I think it's some kind of a call for help, but it might be from anybody in his former unit."

"That's what I want to find out," said Candy. "I have a right to know if he is dead or alive."

"How long has it been since you saw Clem?" I asked her.

She stopped to consider.

"It was about three months before the Americans landed. About a year and a half ago."

"Don't you think, if Clem were still alive, even if he were crippled and sick, that he would have found some way to get in touch with you?"

"I don't know," she sobbed. "I don't know. I don't care about this terrible conspiracy of the collaborators, as you call it. Go to Baguio and look for Clem." She put her arms around my neck, the way she used to do when she was a little girl and wasted my share of the candy. "Please, Gar."

"Give me another week," I told her. "If something doesn't turn up, then I'll go to Baguio."

She wasn't particularly pleased. But I could be stubborn, too. So I stayed on in Manila, hoping for some clue.

But Estara kept talking about her house party. I had already decided to pass on that deal. By this time I realized that I would gain nothing by going with her crowd.

Then one afternoon I came home from the Army-Navy Club. Candy met me at the door in high excitement.

"There's a little urchin here to see you," she said. "He wouldn't tell me what he wanted. He said he was told only to see you."

"Where is he?" I asked.

"In the kitchen."

He was a tattered little urchin with skinny arms and legs. His hair had not seen a barber for ages. He was sitting on a high stool and devouring a plate of rice and fish. He nodded and smiled.

"You the man," he said.

I leaned my elbows on the table to watch him eat.

"How do you know I'm the man, son?" I asked.

"Because you got big ears," he said.

I laughed.

"Okay," I said. "I've got big ears, bigger than anybody else. Now, what is it you want?"

"I can't talk here," he said, nodding towards Candy.

"Oh, she's all right," I said.

The boy shook his head.

"Well!" said Candy, turning to the door. "I won't intrude where I'm not wanted."

I spoke to the boy in Tagalog.

"We're alone now," I said. "Who sent you?"

"Your friend with the pockmarks."

"Yes?" I asked. "What did he say?"

The boy sucked a fishbone noisily. Then he said conspiratorially, "He had found someone you want. I am to take you to him."

"Well, come on," I told him. "We've got to hurry."

"Just a minute," said the boy. He climbed down from the stool and looked at me like a small David about to throw a stone. "There is a little matter of business. Your friend said you would give me money."

I pulled a bill from my pocket and handed it to him. "Okay?"

Without answering, he pocketed the money and grinned.

Candy was not in sight when we left. We took her jeep and started out.

"Where do we go?" I asked the boy.

"The Quiapo," he said.

I remembered the Quiapo from boyhood excursions. It is a big open market where everything is sold in open stalls. Tourists are shocked to see meat hanging in the sun, where dust and flies can settle on it. But we have been eating it all our lives and haven't died yet, or even been violently sick.

When we approached the market, I saw that things had not changed. Pedestrians swarmed all over the street, so that it was almost impossible to get a car through, even if you wore out your horn. Flower peddlers and candy vendors and women bearing baskets of vegetables on their heads walked easily in the crowd, hawking their wares. The familiar smell of fish and fruit was in the air.

I parked the jeep. The little boy led me past stalls of bananas towards the back. Suddenly, he stopped and pointed a dirty finger.

"There's your friend," he said.

It was Goyo. I turned to thank the boy, but he was gone. I went up to Goyo.

"It took you a long time," he said.

"I was out. Have you found the man we want?"

He nodded. "He's shopping. I have been following him. He is over there buying meat."

I looked in the direction he indicated. I saw the back of a tall man with graying hair. There was nothing about him or his clothes that distinguished him from the others. Yes, he was Igorot. He moved his head slightly and I saw the long earring dangling on his right ear with the tiny pouch at the end where the Igorots carry their tobacco or medicine.

Goyo moved towards him. I followed. Then one of those things happened that always seemed to be happening to me. Somebody clapped me on the back.

"Hello," said a familiar cheerful voice. "Are you still cooking?"

I turned my head. Pepe was smiling at me.

Out of the corner of my eye, I saw that Goyo had slid out of sight. I cursed my luck. I liked Pepe. But, of all people in Manila, he was the last one I wanted to see. My quarry was walking away and out of the market.

Goyo must be hiding somewhere in the crowd. I would have to let him follow the man alone. I did not dare take Pepe into my confidence.

A suspicion began to form in my mind. But it was not until Pepe took my arm and propelled me towards the street that my idea crystallized. I was almost sure that it was more than coincidence that had brought him to me.

This was the third time I had been prevented from talking to someone who could help me. Two of these people had been killed to insure their silence. I looked at Pepe now. He was laughing over one of his own jokes, but I noticed that his eyes were appraising me carefully.

I wondered if I were walking arm in arm with a murderer.

# EIGHT

It took me some time to get rid of Pepe. When I was finally free from him, I made for the bar where I usually met Goyo.

I sat around for a couple of hours. I became bored watching the barmaid swatting flies with a crumpled newspaper. I became bored with the cockroaches chasing each other around the walls. I became bored with the place. Finally, I decided to go out and eat. I told the bartender that if anyone came with a message for me to tell him that I would be right back. I decided to eat somewhere in the neighborhood.

But when I was going out the door, I was accosted by a mysterious character wearing pants that defied pressing, a hat that slouched over his eyes, and a sinister fringe around his upper lip that might have been the beginnings of a mustache.

"You Gar Stanley," he said.

His tone put me on the defensive. "What makes you think so?"

"You the American with freckles and big ears," he told me.

I touched my right ear. I would have to tape them back. They might be convenient for Goyo to describe me, but they certainly made me conspicuous.

"What do you have to tell me?" I asked.

"You meet your friend Ching-How," he replied.

"Where in God's name is that?"

"You give me money I show you," said the anonymous character.

I gave him a bill. It certainly cost money for simple comforts in Manila.

55

He was a talkative creature. We took the jeep and he directed me by grunts and groans to the Chinatown section, near the Tondo. When we swept around a narrow corner and down a cobblestone street, he groaned again and motioned with his hand for me to stop. We jerked to the curb. Then I saw Goyo standing in the recess of a door.

A little boy rushed up to me screaming, "I wash your car, Mister. I keep the robbers away for twenty-five centavos. But for fifty centavos I wipe off the dust!"

I gave him a peso. I said. "Do both."

"With my life!" said the boy with a gesture worthy of Olivier in Hamlet.

My anonymous friend disappeared. I walked up to Goyo.

"He went into the place next door," said Goyo with a jerk of his head. "It's an opium den. I don't think they would let you in. We had better wait here for him."

I sighed heavily.

"Better still," said Goyo, "you go into that restaurant across the street and sit by the window. You are an American and too conspicuous on the street."

I took Goyo's advice. I went into the tiny Chinese restaurant and ordered dinner. I had forgotten how much better the Chinese food is in Manila than in other places. Here you find no cheap suey-chow mein-fried shrimp stuff intended for tourists. It is the real McCoy that the Chinese eat themselves.

I became so enthused over my dinner that I almost forgot my errand. Suddenly a shadow fell ominously across my plate. I looked up. I was sitting by the window, so I caught a fleeting glimpse of something white passing out of sight. Then it was gone.

I ran to the door and looked up and down the street. A man in white tropics was crossing the street. There was something in his walk that was quite familiar. He paused in a doorway and lit a cigarette. Then I saw that it was Pepe.

I ran back to my plate, threw a bill on the counter and dashed out again. But Pepe had disappeared. I looked across the street. Goyo was nodding towards the door where Pepe had stopped.

I walked down the street and looked up at the doorway. The letters over the door were Chinese characters. I looked across the street again. Goyo nodded his head vigorously. I entered the door.

I found myself in a hall so dark that I had to use my cigarette lighter. A double line of closed doors lined both sides of the hall. To my right a narrow staircase rose into darkness. I stood listening for any sound that would tell me where Pepe had gone. Everything was quiet with a graveyard stillness.

Then from the door nearest me, I heard a sound like an old-fashioned phonograph being wound up. Then a scratchy needle began to play "Mama Inez." Two pairs of feet began to move around the room.

I knew Pepe had not come here to dance. I tiptoed to the opposite door. I heard the stertorous sighing of a sleeper, climaxed by a sharp snore. Pepe would not come here to sleep, either.

I continued down the hall. One room was empty. In the next a groaning bed told of violent lovemaking. I heard a woman scream, then a man laughing. It was not Pepe's voice.

The girls were talking loudly in another room. I looked through the keyhole. Two naked Chinese girls were sitting on the edge of a bed.

I went back to the end of the hall and started up the stairs. It was the most evil staircase I had ever encountered. The steps were too small and I could hardly get the balls of my feet on them. There was no handrail. The stairs were built between two walls, and became steeper and narrower as I went up. There seemed to be no end to them.

Then I became aware of a foul smell that seemed to be a combination of all the decomposition in Manila. Breathing through my mouth was no good. This was the kind of smell that penetrated even the pores of the skin. My flickering light showed me that I had reached the top step at last, and also the source of the stink. Somebody had left the door of the latrine partly open. This old building had been erected long before anyone ever heard of plumbing. Their arrangements were the old-fashioned variety found mostly in Chinese quarters.

I closed the door of the latrine and went down to the end

of the hall and stuck my head out of the window for a minute. Then I continued my hunt for Pepe.

I found him on the first try. As I looked through the keyhole of the room nearest the window, I caught a flash of his white trousers. That was all I could see. He was standing with his back to the door. Only his legs were visible.

He was talking to someone. I could hear him speaking in a hushed voice. But I could not make out the words. Then I heard a woman's voice. I could not see the woman.

I went back to the window and looked out. In the dim light of my lighter, I saw a wall that ended in a flat roof. It was so close that I could reach out and touch it. A very narrow ledge extended outside the window to the window of the room in which Pepe was visiting. I took off my shoes, tied the strings together and hung them around my neck. Then I climbed out on the ledge.

It was narrower than my feet. I made it, but I had to cling to the wall of the other building.

I peered in through the window. I could not see inside the entire room. But I could see enough to size up the whole situation.

A young woman with slant eyes was talking to Pepe. I could see at once there was no romance involved. As I watched them, she took off one of her slippers and extracted a slip of paper from the sole and handed it to him. He read the paper, smiled, and nodded. I craned my neck to see what was on the paper but it was too far away. Pepe folded the paper again and put it in his inside coat pocket. They talked for a few minutes longer. Then he bowed and left.

It was when he was leaving that I saw the two other men. Apparently they had been standing near the door, out of the range of my vision. They were tough-looking fellows, not quite as big as Primo Carnera. They looked like bodyguards.

It was time for me to duck out and go after Pepe. I had to get that paper. I was convinced now that he was definitely tied up in some racket.

Again it was my bad luck that decided things for me. I had plenty of luck in this business and all of it seemed to be bad.

My shoestring became loose and my left shoe fell to the ground. I managed to retain the other. Why I bothered, I don't know. One shoe is no good to anybody.

The remaining shoe banged against the window. In the room, startled eyes stared out at me. One of the men started towards the window. I plunged to the opposite wall, then climbed to the roof of the building.

I saw the man reach inside his jacket. I fell flat before he fired. He fired twice. They both went wild. He and his pal made for the door.

I started running across the roof. It was a flat, tin-roofed building, littered with bits of broken glass and boards with nails and bits of rocks. I stepped on them all in my stockinged feet. I ran across the roof wildly, looking for a getaway. I saw the two men climbing up the wall. I swung down on the far side and sidled along on my hands until I found an open window.

I swung into a dark room and stumbled around searching for the door. My entrance disturbed another couple making love under a net. The woman screamed. The man jumped off the bed after me. I found the door, unlocked it, and ran out.

The stairs were just outside the room. I started down. Sounds of violence came to me from the room I had just left. Then the door was thrust open and one of the gunsels was coming after me.

I jumped the rest of the way, landed on the floor on my shoulder, picked myself up and plunged out into the street. I cursed myself for not bringing my gun.

Goyo was gone from his place. The little boy was still watching my jeep, but I dared not go after it. I ran down the street, swung around a corner, and dived into the first doorway. My pursuers came charging around the corner and down an alley and emerged on another street. They were gaining on me. Once or twice they fired, but the street was too dark to hit a target.

I was panting heavily and knew I would have to take refuge quickly. Then I saw the church across the street. The lights were on.

I made for the door and stopped for a moment. My pursuers were now in sight. They ran towards me with drawn guns.

I slipped inside the door and leaned heavily against the wall so that I could keep an eye on the street. I saw them come up the steps, putting back the guns in their pockets.

I looked around for another door. There was one on the

side well towards the front. Some of the faithful were crawling along the aisle on their knees. It is one's self-imposed penance. I joined the procession and found myself between two withered old ladies wearing black shawls on their heads. I made my way up to the front on my knees, then stood up and crawled into a pew. For a minute, I felt safe under the eyes of the padre and the congregation.

Then somebody had joined me. One of them was behind me. I could feel his gun poking my ribs. The other took my arm and hung on, while he looked ahead and nodded his head gravely at the solemn drama on the altar. I could feel his gun in my back.

# NINE

I hated to see the evening services end. I watched the congregation filing out, and my mind turned somersaults. There was no doubt but that the two gunsels intended to let me have it as soon as we were outside.

The one on my right, whom I had privately named Bruiser, started pulling at my arm. The other, Killer, was tickling my ribs with his gun. There was no escape. I had to get up and start off with the crowd. Bruiser held my arm in a death grip and Killer walked so close behind me that he stumbled on my heels.

When we approached the entrance my hope was rapidly diminishing. The faithful were dipping their hands in the fountain of holy water. A few old women in black shawls were clustering around the padre at the door. I decided to take a chance. It was probably my last chance, anyway.

When we walked past the priest, I suddenly shot out my hand and grasped his firmly.

"Hello, Father," I said. "I haven't seen you in years." The padre allowed himself to reflect surprise for a minute, then he smiled and shook my hand. If he understood the situation, he did not show it.

"Maybe you don't remember me," I went on desperately. "I used to attend your church, but I was away for some time."

"I'm very glad to see you back," answered the priest.

I was trying to think of something else to say, anything to engage his attention. Then an old lady said something to him and he turned away. Bruiser was tugging at my arm. Killer was growling at me. There was only one thing left.

"By the way, Father," I said loudly. "I would like to make a little donation to your church."

It worked. Money is always a miracle worker. He was all smiles.

"I would like to give you a check," I said. "Could we go into your office?"

"Yes, certainly," he answered. He bowed goodnight to his parishioners. He laid his hand on my arm and said, "I'm glad you came back."

Bruiser was forced to relinquish his claim on me. Killer was flabbergasted. They followed us to the perch. At the door, I turned to them.

"You wait here," I said. Then I slipped inside and the priest swiftly bolted the door.

The priest must have noticed my hurry to get inside. He probably saw my stockinged feet. But he said nothing. He led me into his office and indicated a chair. I mopped the perspiration off my face.

"It's a warm night," said the priest.

"It's a very warm night," I agreed.

"Would you like a glass of water?" he asked.

When he turned his back to get the water, I lit a cigarette. I did not want him to see that my hands were shaking. I drank the water he handed me and wrote him a check.

"This is very kind of you," he said, beaming over the check. "This will help us to restore some broken windows."

"This is very kind of you, too," I said.

Outside everything was quiet. Too quiet. I went to the window and looked out. Bruiser was standing at the foot of the steps, watching the front door. Killer was not in sight. I looked back at the priest.

"Conditions are very unsettled here," he said. "The poverty and hardship induced by the war have left the city in a restless state. A stranger is scarcely safe on the streets at night."

"Yes," I said, "there are times when a man can't even call on the police for help. Things are going on which involve people in high circles."

"A very sad state of affairs," commended the padre. Then he added, as if changing the subject, "By the way, have you ever seen my garden? It is a closed-in garden which leads directly to the church and is very beautiful in the moonlight."

"A closed-in garden, Father?" I asked.

"It is surrounded by high walls," he said.

"I would certainly like to see your garden," I said.

I followed him to another room which opened out into a private yard. For a moment I paused, looking outside. The moon laid a tracery through the branches of trees [indecipherable text] walk that led across the garden. On another side of the walk, dark forms of bushes and plants hunched in the shadows like watchful gnomes. The heavy scent of ilang-ilang sweetened the air.

I followed the priest along the path, hugging the shadows of the thick foliage.

We were nearing the entrance to the church when I saw the figure standing half-hidden by a banyan tree. I halted abruptly and, touching the priest's arm, pointed towards the figure.

He looked in the direction I indicated, nodded his head and whispered in my ear. "That is the statue of Saint Anthony. I think you can trust him."

He opened the heavy side door. I followed him back into the church. Within the church it was completely dark now except for the red glow of a candle on the altar. The air was aromatic from incense and flowers. We walked across the center of the church to the other side. The priest paused at another door and slid back the bolt.

"This door opens on another street," he whispered.

"Thank you very much, Father," I said.

He peered at me in the dim light.

"Thank you also, son," he said. "Thank you for not causing a commotion in my church. Go with God."

I grinned and he shut the door. He was a wise old padre.

I took a circuitous route back to my jeep. When I was within sight of it, I heard the motor of an approaching car. I dodged in the shadow of a doorway and waited. A long, low-slung car drew up. It halted in front of the building where I had followed Pepe.

Bruiser got out of the car and went inside the building. Killer remained at the wheel. Bruiser did not stay inside long. He came out with a woman. She walked up to Killer. Then I heard a loud smack.

"You fool!" she said. "Take me to the Club if you can find it!"

Bruiser held the door for her. He climbed in front beside Killer. They drove away.

When they were gone, I climbed into my jeep. I started after them. I put my hat on and also a pair of dark glasses. It wasn't much of a disguise but it might keep them from recognizing me. I trailed after them down Quezon Boulevard. Then they swung down España and I followed them to the edge of Quezon City. There, set in a small, parklike enclosure, I saw the blue lights of the Linda Mujer Nightclub.

I watched Bruiser help the woman out of the car. The doorman bowed to her. She sailed inside like Queen Mary taking Buckingham Palace. Killer drove the car towards the back of the club. I was about to pull into the parking lot when I remembered that something essential was missing.

I had forgotten that I had no shoes.

# TEN

It was unavoidable. Even in Manila where nearly everything goes, a man cannot walk into a nightclub without his shoes unless he expects to arouse comment.

I swung the jeep around and headed for home. When I entered the house, Candy was sitting by herself in the sala. She was playing solitaire. She took one look at me and cried, "Where are your shoes?"

"I gave them away," I said. "Got a drink?"

"I'll get some ice," she said.

"Never mind the ice, just bring me the bottle," I told her. I poured half a glassful and drained it.

Candy curled up beside me on the sofa. "What happened tonight?" she asked.

"Plenty, but I haven't time to tell you now. I'm on a hot trail and I just came home to get my shoes."

"You're always on a hot trail," said Candy, following me upstairs. "But it never leads anywhere. Where are you going now?"

"I'm going to a nightclub," I said. I turned and leered at her. "I'm going to meet a beautiful wicked woman."

"I'm going with you," said Candy.

"No, it's better if I go alone," I told her.

"You always say that. And all you ever do is get into trouble. This time I'm coming with you. You needn't shout. It won't do you any good."

"Okay," I conceded. "Grab your scarf or something while I change. But don't complain if I neglect you."

"Don't worry about me," said Candy. "I'm never neglected in a nightclub."

I hurriedly changed into another suit. I slipped my gun in my pocket.

Candy was waiting for me when I went downstairs. I looked at her and whistled. She had on some filmy stuff that blended from pale pink to deep violet, with plenty of skirt and very little above the waist. Candy could get away with that kind of dress. She had plenty of figure in the right places.

On my way to the nightclub, I told Candy about the evening's events. I did not, however, tell Candy that I had seen the woman hand Pepe the slip of paper. I was afraid if Candy knew about it she might try a little detective work on her own and get herself in a kettle of trouble. I only told Candy that I had seen Pepe talking to the woman, and the consequences of my spying.

"You are certainly turning out to be a super snooper," she commented. "Why are you walking into their trap?"

"Because I want to find out where this woman fits into the picture. Have you ever heard of her?"

Candy shrugged. "How can I tell until I see her? From your description, she must be part Chinese. That would apply to hundreds of women in Manila."

I swung around a curve. "She ain't hundreds," I said. "Not even Manila could hold more than one like her."

"That's what I like about you," said Candy. "You never look at another woman."

"There was a time," I reminded her, "when I wouldn't have."

We bumped along over the uneven road in silence for a few minutes. Then Candy said, "I'm sorry, Gar. I didn't have any right to say that. I really don't have any claims on you, do I?"

She pulled a cigarette out of her case. I flicked my lighter for her.

"We can't talk about that," I told her, "until we find out about Clem."

Candy puffed in silence for a moment. Then she asked, "Do you think there will be more trouble tonight?"

"I wouldn't be surprised," I said. "But now I'm prepared for it." I patted my hip pocket. "If I should disappear, don't start a riot. Wait a while and if I don't show up, just go home like a good girl."

Linda Mujer turned out to be a nightclub with a lively Cuban band where everybody jumped around in the latest jungle dances and shouted a lot of "Ai-ai-ais." We took a table and had a couple of drinks while we looked around for some lead. The woman with the slant eyes was not in sight. I noticed that a number of couples entered the front door and went directly to another room at the back. I signaled the waiter and asked for our bill.

"You are leaving so soon?" he asked. "The floor show will be on in a few minutes."

"We are going into the casino for a while," I told him, slipping him five pesos. I knew a place like this was bound to have a casino.

"Yes, sir," said the waiter pocketing the tip. He bowed to us like a padre giving benediction. "It is on your left."

We had no trouble finding the casino. The door was guarded by none other than my pal Bruiser.

He stiffened when he saw me. His hand jerked towards his left breastpocket. Then his arm dropped back to his side. He could hardly shoot me in full view of a dozen people. He opened the door.

Roulette and fantan seemed to be the most popular games in the casino. There was some version of black jack going on, but I didn't pay much attention to it. Candy and I made for the roulette table.

The Woman was there. She was not playing. She was walking around the room and talking to some of the players. This was my first good look at her. She was very small, with tiny hands and shiny jetblack hair and dead white skin. But it was her eyes that were arresting.

I could see now that they were not really slant, but elongated and tilted upwards at the corners. They were the kind of eyes that would make her a fortune anywhere. She must have been wearing something, but I didn't notice it. I was completely absorbed by the contrast of her big eyes against the thick whiteness of her skin and the flaming red curve of her mouth.

"Are you here with me or are you at a movie?" whispered Candy.

"That's the woman," I told her. I placed a bet.

"Anybody could see that," said Candy. "You look like a schoolboy at your first burlesque."

I spoke to the man playing next to me.

"Who is that woman who seems to be the hostess?" I asked.

"Oh, don't you know Rosa Linkhow?" he replied. "She owns this club." He winked at me. "She's the querida of Montalvo."

"Montalvo the banker?" I asked, pulling in my chips. For some reason I had won, although I had no idea what I had bet.

"That's the one," said the man.

I placed another bet and ordered drinks for Candy and me. Things were beginning to shape up, after all. I had been hobnobbing with the wrong branch of the Moltavos, that was all. I should have known that a man like Montalvo would have a querida, otherwise known as a wife-on-the-side, and that she would be deeper in his secrets than his own wife.

I watched Rosa go through a door, pass behind the cashier's cage and disappeared. I pushed the remainder of my chips over to Candy and whispered for her to wait.

I went up to the cashier's cage and asked them to cash a check. The cashier looked at the check for a minute, then he got up from his stool and went through another door. In a few minutes, he returned to the window.

"Would you mind stepping through the door on your right, please?" He indicated a door. "This way, sir."

As I approached the door, I heard a buzzer. I pushed the door open and walked into Rosa Linkhow's office.

She was sitting behind an enormous carved teakwood desk. The desk made her look tinier than ever. As I entered she looked up, slowly rose to her feet, walked around the desk and leaned against it while she surveyed me in amusement.

"I see that you have found your shoes," she said. She had a drawling cool voice, like a frozen mountain stream that is beginning to thaw.

"I couldn't come to see you without them," I said.

Other women smiled by stretching their lips tight against their teeth. Rosa Linkhow merely pouted her lips together, but somehow she made the act more significant.

"Of course not," she drawled. She handed me back my

check and moved across the room with a sinuous grace. "The cashier will take care of your check." She leaned back on the divan and patted the cushion beside her. "Sit down and tell me what you are looking for tonight."

"That was a fool thing to do," I admitted, taking out my cigarette case. "I was looking for a friend of mine and as I passed that room, I thought I heard his voice."

"Did you find your friend?"

"No," I lied. "I must have made a mistake."

She rose and went to a cabinet and took out a bottle and glasses.

"Ice?"

"No thanks."

She brought the bottle and glasses to the coffee table and carefully poured a pair of drinks. I noticed the label. Courvoisier.

"It is very risky to go about Manila looking in windows," said Rosa slowly, sipping her drink. "One might learn things that are too dangerous to know."

"Dangerous for whom?" I asked. "For the one who looks, or the one who is looked at?"

She eyed me speculatively. "It is dangerous for the one who looks," she said. "He is apt to misunderstand what he sees."

"A woman like you has many secrets," I replied. "But it wasn't your secrets that brought me here tonight?"

"No? What was it?"

I regarded her a moment before I answered.

"I wanted to see what lay behind your eyes."

She pouted her lips again and leaned towards me. "Yes? And have you found what you wanted?"

I shook my head. "The answer isn't that simple."

She raised her glass to her lips and tilted it until all I could see were her great dark eyes fastened on me. She put her glass down and smiled at me, this time displaying a row of small white teeth.

"You are right," said Rosa. "Nothing in the Orient is simple. In your country it is different. When a man and woman are friends, they share each other's secrets. But here, one cannot always know one's friends. For instance, you. How can I tell if you are a friend?"

"Try me," I invited.

She leaned towards me on one hip. She put my arm around her and leaned her head against my shoulder, looking up at me with her expressionless eyes.

"Is this the way it is done?" she asked softly.

I drew her closer. "It's a good beginning," I said.

She laughed. Then she frowned a little and rubbed her finger against the spot where my gun was concealed.

"In your Wild West," said Rosa, "isn't it the custom to park the guns when you dance?"

"I wasn't sure what kind of a dance we were going to have," I told her.

Suddenly she leaned across me, putting one arm around my neck while her other hand dangled over the back of the divan.

"What a strange man you are," she murmured. "Reckless on one hand, and overcautious on the other. Do you always go visiting women with a gun?"

Before I could answer I heard the sound of the buzzer. I understood now why Rosa's fingers had lain carelessly on the edge of the divan. There was another electric button concealed there. My head jerked up. Bruiser was coming in the door. He paused behind us.

"Is this one of the men who chased you tonight?" asked Rosa without changing her position.

"Right."

She nodded her head sadly. Then she looked at Bruiser and suddenly barked, "Let him have it!"

I ducked, spilling her to the floor as I reached for my gun, but Bruiser's hand was quicker. Something hit my head. I dropped to my knees, still fumbling for my gun.

"You cheap Romeo," I heard Rosa say, "I almost believed you till I found your gun."

I had the gun in my hand now and started to swing around when Bruiser slugged me again. I felt my nose hit the carpet. And then I was lost in the deep darkness of unconsciousness.

# ELEVEN

Now something was burning. At first I thought I had died and gone to Heaven and then I remembered they didn't burn things in Heaven, so then I decided maybe I had died and gone to the wrong place.

I tried opening my eyes, half-prepared to see little demons with tails wagging, and pitch folks. The demons were there all right, but I couldn't see them. They were prodding the top of my head with sharp spikes and burning my eyeballs, probably with their little wagging tails. I groaned and turned my head. It was a mistake. One little demon plopped down on the top of my skull and thumped his heels against my forehead. I closed my eyes and groaned again.

A woman's voice said, "He's coming around."

Yes, something was burning. The smell was coming closer. I remembered that I was a big brave boy now, so I tried to open one eye again, determined to see the lady demon who was sharing my afterlife with me.

It was no lady. It was a cigar.

My eyes found the glowing tip of the cigar hovering over me, then the hand behind the cigar. It was a deep unctuous voice, like gears that had just been coiled.

I looked for the cigar again. It had moved upward, past the body of a big man and into a face. I looked back. The face fitted the voice. It had big pouchy brown cheeks and cute little piggish eyes that squinted at me from between slits of fat flesh. The hand with the ring touched my shoulder.

"Do you think you can sit up now?" asked the voice.

I took a breath and raised myself painfully. I was on a

sofa. I swung my legs onto the floor and held my head between my hands. Whirling waves of nausea blacked me out for a minute.

"Rosa, bring some coffee and brandy," said the voice.

It was not unctuous now. It was masterful and commanding.

Somebody held a cup of coffee under my nose. It was a woman's hand with long red fingernails. In her other hand was a pony of brandy. I reached for the brandy and poured it into my mouth, feeling it smart all the way down. It hit my stomach and bounced back up to my head. I shuddered and felt better. My hands were steady now. I reached for the coffee without rattling he cup. I gulped some of it down, then I looked at the two people in front of me.

The man sat in a chair opposite me. He crossed one leg over the other. He was dripping cigar ashes onto the parquet floor. Rosa Linkhow sat quietly on a hassock. She did not look nearly as fascinating to me now. I could even see that there were little lines around her eyes.

The man must be Papa Montalvo, I thought. I looked again at him and saw in his face a reflection of what his sons would be like in twenty years.

"I cannot sufficiently apologize for what happened to you tonight, Mr. Stanley," said Montalvo. "I was thoroughly annoyed when I learned how you had been manhandled."

"Shall we say it was abrupt?" I suggested.

Rosa folded and unfolded her hands.

"I do hope you will forgive me, Mr. Stanley," she said, and now her voice was like a plaintive little bell. "When you came to my office, I had no idea what your intentions were. Strangers use many pretexts to hold up people. I did not know then that you were a friend of Mr. Montalvo."

"How did you find out?" I asked.

"Your friend, Mrs. Mayo, became worried about you and telephoned me," Montalvo said.

I had forgotten all about poor Candy.

"Where is she now?" I asked.

"I had someone drive her home," said Montalvo. "I had you brought here to Rosa's house because I wanted a chance to get acquainted with you without interruption." He turned abruptly to Rosa. "Leave us alone," he said.

I watched Rosa walk meekly out of the room. The tigress had become a mouse. This Montalvo must be quite a tamer. When we were alone he pulled his chair a little closer and leaned forward with his elbows on his knees.

Here it comes, I thought. A nice chitchat. Everything as cozy and sociable as if we were at the Army-Navy Club.

"I have wanted to become acquainted with you for some time," Montalvo began confidentially. "My family admire you very much." His tone held just that right degree of a sly joke between men. He leaned back in his chair, puffing on his cigar, expensive and important, but not condescending. Oh, no. He was too smooth for that. Sometimes you pity these smooth guys who could have done something constructive for their people.

"We have been through a bad time in this country," he continued. "In addition to the ravages of war, we are now an independent country and no longer under the protection of the United States." He began to warm up and his voice vibrated with earnestness as he told me, "It is only through the cooperation of men like yourself, Mr. Stanley, that we can hope to plant the seeds of prosperity and watch our land blossom into a flower of democracy."

He paused, as if waiting for station identification. I wondered if I was supposed to applaud. He ought to run for Congress, I thought. He'd be sure of his own vote. Maybe if I kept still and let him run down we'd get to the point of all this verbal hide-and-seek. I began to suspect that his speech was a buildup to offering me Estara's heart and hand. But his next words jolted me a little.

"We all remember your father well, Mr. Stanley. The gold mine in which he owned a share helped tremendously toward the making of our prosperity. But your father is gone. His friend Mr. Mayo, who owned the other portion, is also dead. What are your plans for the mine?"

I sat back and lit a cigarette on that one. If the old boy knew so much, he must also know that I had no money to reopen the mine. If he was working up to an offer of financing me, he must be in this pretty deep. Gold mines are not put to work on ten centavos.

I shrugged. "Everyone knows I'm broke," I said.

"As a banker and a patriot," said Montalvo, watching the end of this cigar, "I feel it my duty to assist you in reopening the mine. Hundreds of people would be put to work that are now unemployed. That is a point worth considering."

"What kind of assistance did you have mind?" I asked.

"A private loan," replied Montalvo. "At a low rate of interest." He broke off as if he were about to add something else, but wanted his words to sink in my mind first. They sunk.

"What else?" I asked.

He smiled gently as if he had been waiting for that question. He stared dreamily at a point beyond my shoulder.

"The world is still quaking from the repercussions of war, Mr. Stanley," he began. "You have been away a long time. No doubt you have seen evidences of change since you returned. There are vile forces at work, seeking to undermine men of character and authority. We must stamp them out, Mr. Stanley." He finally focused his eyes on mine. They were still small and piggish eyes. "A man like yourself is apt to be mistaken in his sympathies because he is unacquainted with the whole structure of the case." His voice became gentle, almost caressing, as he added, "That is why, Mr. Stanley, we must insist on settling our own affairs in our way, since it is only we who are acquainted with all of the facts."

What a rigamarole of words, I thought. Brother, you are scared. I wonder what Clem has on you. It must be something terrific.

"I'll think over your offer," I told him.

"Think it over carefully," he said, and smiled. "We must all hang together in these uncertain times."

"Or hang separately?" I asked.

He regarded me sharply for a minute, then smiled again, and his face rolled up into innumerable folds.

"You Americans and your jokes," he remonstrated gently. "But one word of advice, Mr. Stanley. Times are uncertain in Manila. Men have been kidnapped and never heard of again. Others have had accidents and their assailants were never caught. I suggest that you move very carefully in the future and choose your company."

Yes, it was plain enough. Either I played on his team or

my name went in his little black book. American gangster movies had apparently educated Manila, too. This was my cue, I knew, to stand up like Trueblue Harold and wave my arms and tell him to shoot if he must my old gray head. But I couldn't. The cards were all stacked in his favor and I did not have a single clue to work on. I felt defeated.

Then I remembered the war and I thought of the thousands of little people that had suffered hunger and privation while a few like Montalvo grew rich and fat in the midst of that suffering. Every country had its Quislings, every nation its collaborators. And that was what the War Crimes Trials were for—to make the world free from traitors and selfish opportunists. And I remembered also the hell I had gone through in North Africa, the endless marching under a blistering sun with the taste of sand and dust in my eyes and mouth, and I remembered being hungry and thirsty and afraid to die. And I thought, Hell! I belong with the other little people and our war isn't over yet.

So I said, "I've made up my mind about your offer, Montalvo. I have other business to finish before I can think of reopening the mine."

He took it in a friendly way. He stood up and looked at me almost tenderly and shook his head.

"I'm very sorry to hear your unwise decision," he said softly. He walked swiftly to a door, opened it and jerked his head.

My two old friends, Bruiser and Killer, entered the room. They looked expectant. I got up. Montalvo shook his head at me.

"I wouldn't do anything if I were you," he said. "My men are armed. They are going to take you for a little trip to the country. I will be out and see you in a few days and I am sure by that time you will have changed your mind." I started for the window, but Bruiser caught me halfway across the room. Killer had his gun out, revolving it in his hand in a bad imitation of Billy the Kid.

Bruiser pinned my hands behind my back. They marched me to the front door. Montalvo disappeared into another room. When they opened the door, I saw the first gray streaks of dawn in the sky. Montalvo's long black car was parked in front of the house. A chauffeur was waiting at the wheel.

I tried to wrench my arms free, but Bruiser clipped me on

the chin. They hauled me into the car and pushed me into the back seat, one guard on either side of me.

I thought, this is it. This is the end of the North Africa march. This is the end of the sand and dust and being thirsty. This is the end of my war.

The car started. My jaw ached. Then we stopped with a jerk. The chauffeur kept pushing his foot on the starter and the engine rumbled, but the car did not move. The motor was flooded. I looked at the chauffeur when he got out of the car and lifted the hood of the motor. Then I saw something that wrenched me back into full consciousness.

As the chauffeur bent over the engine, I saw, dangling from his ear, a long earring with the little pouch at the end.

I had found my man.

# TWELVE

The driver finally got the car started. We bumped along the unpaved road until we hit a boulevard. Reaction from tension set in on me. Maybe it was because of my relief at finding the man with the earring after chasing him all over Manila. Maybe it was simply that I was tired from being knocked around twice in one night.

Anyway, I fell asleep.

I was finally awakened by the heat and the jerking car. We had hit another unpaved section of road. I looked around for familiar landmarks. But I discovered that I had been away from the Philippines too long and forgotten my geography. The countryside was a flat riceland, broken by groves of coconut and nipa palms.

When we passed through villages, I saw the same little nipa shacks that I had seen in all villages. They clustered at the edge of the road like dried giant mushrooms.

We turned off the main road onto a side land which had apparently been meant only for oxcarts. We thumped over it at about five miles an hour. I could feel the car hit each ridge and I prayed fervently for a broken axle. But the department that listened to prayers wasn't open for business yet, because we emerged from this patch of road with only bugs smashed on the windshield.

Then the car suddenly came to a halt. I looked around, wondering why. There was no habitation in sight, nothing but a sugar cane plantation on one side of the road and what looked like a deep ravine on the other.

Bruiser and Killer hauled me out of the car. The man with the earring remained at the wheel. He did not glance at me.

"What happens now?" I asked Bruiser.

He jerked his head towards the ravine. "We go over the bridge."

I swung my head around towards the chauffeur. I tried desperately to catch his eye. He was a big Igorot, all right, with the high-bridged nose and sharp cheekbones and impenetrable expression of the American Indian. He glanced at me once, then started the motor.

I couldn't believe it. I knew it was no use calling out to him for help. But I had thought that, surely, somewhere along the trip, he would have managed an accident or any slight mishap to give me a break. Bruiser jerked my arm.

They pulled me across the road and through the wild grass that grew knee-high. I heard the car disappearing in the distance. My last hope was gone.

Then I saw the bridge. It was a long narrow bamboo without side rails, stretching across the ravine. It creaked and swayed like a willow.

I was frankly terrified. The corners of Bruiser's mouth jerked upward. Maybe it was meant to be a smile, or maybe it was the way he had learned to sneer from Edward G. Robinson movies. He nodded his head and prodded me in the small of my back.

Well, I thought, I'll start a rumpus on the bridge. At least we'll all land in the water. But at the edge of the ravine, I realized again that my department in heaven was still closed. There was no water. There may have been water here a million years ago, but it was now only a rocky gorge of volcanic lava.

I had a fair idea where we were now. We were south of Manila, where there is a volcano called Mount Taal that still sends up occasional smoke signals. I looked around hopefully. I would have settled for even a very small eruption. But there was no smoke today. Even the volcano wouldn't help me.

Killer tied a stout rope around my waist. I couldn't see how the rope would help me. I saw Bruiser start out across the bridge. It took him a long time. But once on the other side, he tied one end of the rope to a tree. He nodded towards me. It was my turn now.

I stepped on the bridge, holding the rope. The bridge swayed and creaked. I began to appreciate the rope. I would certainly have lost my balance if I had not been tied to it. I was perspiring when I reached the other side. It was the one and only time that I was glad of Bruiser's existence.

I turned and watch Killer. I hoped the bridge would collapse under his weight. But he was even more skilled than Bruiser. He came forward easily and with great confidence, walking as if he were on the broad streets of Manila.

Then I noticed that we were at the entrance of a big hacienda. I could see numerous workers in a sugarcane field. Several half-starved dogs leaped towards us, yelping and growling. Bruiser growled back and they slunk away.

They did not take me to the main house. They hauled me around to the back where I saw many little shacks where the workers lived. I could hear the noise of a generating plant.

We went around behind the plant to a little wooden shed. There was a wooden ladder leading up to the door.

They took me up the ladder and opened the door. We were greeted by the hot dry smell of a long closed-in room. I heard the rustle of wings. Bats flew close to our heads.

They pushed me into a chair and bound me tight with ropes.

"You stay here," Bruiser said, unnecessarily, I thought. He slapped me sharply in the face.

I bit his thumb.

"Son-of-a-bitch!" he yelled.

He whanged me hard across the mouth.

I saw Killer's fist coming. I turned my head away. He grabbed my ears and banged my head against the back of the chair.

Killer could have been called the Sandman. He always put me to sleep.

# THIRTEEN

The bats and rats had quite a day. I emerged from the sleep that Killer had slugged me into, and became conscious of a terrific heat. I thought at first that the place was on fire. Something scurried around my feet. It was a big rat, almost the size of a full-grown cat.

Perspiration streamed down my cheeks. The salt from the perspiration stung my cut lips. I tried to lick it away. My fingers tingled and my legs ached. And I was thirsty.

I saw a crack of gray light under the door. I had been unconscious most of the day, because the gray light meant evening. I wondered if Bruiser and Killer had come back and slugged me again when I was unconscious.

The heat was the worst. There were no windows in the shed. The blistering heat clung to the walls, soaking up whatever air there might have been. I tried hard to breathe. My throat ached.

Then I heard heavy footsteps mounting the ladder. The door opened. My one good eye focused on the figure of either Bruiser or Killer, I couldn't tell which. I didn't give a damn either. He was carrying a jug.

"Water," I groaned.

"I give you water," he said.

He did. He emptied the jug over my head. It was the most humane thing he had done. Some of it dripped into the edges of my mouth. The rest of it soaked my head and dripped down my burning shoulders.

He examined my bindings and poked my face around a couple of times. I went back to sleep.

When I awoke again it was already dark. I saw a slit of

moonlight under the door. Crickets were singing somewhere in the night. My body was burning with pain. And I did not know how long this torture would go on. I was almost willing to die.

Then I heard a faint rustle. I thought it came from the bats. Then I saw the door was slowly opening. It couldn't have been Bruiser. Or Killer. Their footsteps always gave them away. They walked like drugged horses.

The door continued to open until the moonlight revealed the outline of a tall thin man. He was barefoot. He glided swiftly forward and bent over me. It was the man with the earring, the Igorot who had brought us to the place. He touched my bruised cheeks and lips with his finger and grunted softly. He cut my bindings with a knife that flashed whitely in the moonlit room.

I tried to stand up, but my legs were weak. He took off my shoes and massaged my ankles and wrists until the circulation came back. Then he helped me to my feet. He tied my shoes around my neck and, with one arm around me, led me towards the door. The fresh air smelled so good that for a moment I was giddy.

We took a circuitous route through the fields of sugarcane. The soft trenches of earth felt good under my bare feet. The heat of the night was still oppressive. But suddenly the moon disappeared and a streak of lightning leaped across the sky. There was a loud clap of thunder and another flash of lightning, and it began to rain when we reached the bridge.

I hesitated at the foot of the bridge, wondering how I was going to cross it. But the Igorot showed me how. We sat down and pushed ourselves along with our hands. Even so, it was rough going. I was still weak, and waves of dizziness hit me. I looked straight ahead, not down into the ravine. We finally made it.

I crawled onto a high tuft of grass. I lay down breathing hard, letting the soft rain soak into me. The Igorot helped me up and motioned for me to put on my shoes. I looked over towards the valley and saw the hacienda glowing in the thick darkness.

Then I remembered about this place. I had heard about it from a Filipino student named Claro that I had known at Columbia University. He had worked here as a boy. It had been a regular slave labor camp then, where the workers were paid twenty-five centavos a day. All living expenses were deducted from their pay, so that at the end of the month they had very little coming, and sometimes nothing. The bridge was built to make it hard for them to escape.

Well, Claro had escaped. And so had I. I felt that I had set a precedent for these poor guys that worked here. When they learned that I had escaped, maybe they would start running away, too. I thumbed my nose at the bridge and stood up and followed the Igorot down the road.

I stumbled in the mud. But it didn't matter. I was free. I squinted as the figure of my guide merged into the darkness. I hurried along after him. Finally he stopped. When I came up to him, I saw that he was standing beside a small car. I almost bumped into it. When he opened the door, I saw another man inside. I peered at him.

"Hello," said Goyo's voice. "How do you feel now?"

I sighed. I was so glad to hear Goyo's voice that I could have thrown my arms around him. I climbed in and sat beside him. The Igorot got in through the other door and started the motor.

"That was some clambake," I said.

"You hungry?" asked Goyo. He shoved something wrapped in banana leaves into my hand. "Here's some rice cakes and bananas."

I devoured the meal, even part of the banana leaves. Goyo gave me a cigarette. I puffed for a few minutes.

Then I leaned forward and said to the Igorot, "I thought you turned me down this morning."

The Igorot grunted and grinned.

"He can't talk," said Goyo.

"Can't talk!" I repeated.

"The Japs cut off the end of his tongue." Goyo explained. "We were in Fort Santiago together. We took care of each other. They didn't hurt me so bad, only my fingernails. But he had a bad time. That's why he's working in the underground now to round up the collaborators."

"What's his name?" I asked Goyo.

"Damyan," answered Goyo. "He is from the mountain country. Damyan had to be sure of you before he would help. When he saw you go with Montalvo's thugs this morning, he knew that you were all right."

I was relieved. If Damyan were on my side, at last I knew I would eventually solve the mystery surrounding Clem.

"Where are we going now?" I asked.

"Damyan thinks you should go to Baguio to hunt for the man who sent you the ring. He will give you a paper to show to a man up there who will help you. Damyan cannot take you all the way up. He has some work here to do. And then, too." Goyo added with a shrug, "the man who owns this car may soon discover his loss."

I looked at him with some doubt.

"Oh, it is easy to pick up a car in Manila," said Goyo. "When a man parks his car to go into a restaurant, you bump into him as soon as he steps on the sidewalk, and if you are a clever pickpocket like me, you take his keys. Then in a few minutes you bribe the boy who watches this car to go away. It is simple."

I laughed. "You stole this car?"

"Oh, no," said Goyo. "Anything that is stolen is not returned. We only borrowed it. It will be left on a street where it can easily be found."

I patted Goyo's shoulder. "I'm surely glad we're on the same team."

The rain had stopped. We were speeding down a smooth section of the road now. I saw the speedometer register eighty. There were no other cars on the road. Nobody over here travels the highways at night except in case of extreme urgency.

"How far is Damyan taking me?" I asked.

"Pampanga. You will be met there by someone who will take you to the mountains."

"This deal seems to be well organized," I commented. "How does Damyan make himself understood if he cannot talk?"

"Oh, he writes a little, and I read a little," said Goyo. "He is making me his assistant."

"Good for you, Goyo," I said. "Do you get a salary?"

He shook his head sadly.

I dug into my pocket and pulled out a few peso bills.

"Maybe this will help you." I said.

"Thank you, Mr. Gar," said Goyo, pocketing the bills. "It is a pleasure to do business with you."

I slid down in the seat and dozed off and did not awaken until we hit rough road.

"We are now at the bridge of Pampanga Province," said Goyo.

The headlight beamed on a narrow one-way suspension bridge that had been damaged in the war. It was hastily rebuilt with loose wooden boards. I saw the lights of a small constabulary depot. When we had crossed the bridge, the highway became smooth again, curving and dipping around the hills. We drove about a mile further. Then Damyan stopped the car beside a cluster of tamarind trees and turned off the headlights. I peered outside, but the night was black. I could not see anything.

"It looks like nobody is here yet," I said.

"Damyan will call them," whispered Goyo.

Damyan took a reed flute out of his pocket and put it to his nose. A few notes of weird music floated in the night. It was the same music that I had heard in the Tondo district of Manila, the night that Agna, the nightclub singer, had been killed.

"So that's his signal," I said. "If I had known that, I would have found him sooner."

"The mountain people have strange ways," said Goyo.

I saw a gleam ahead of us, as if a match had been struck and then blown out. Damyan answered the signal with his headlights. In the sudden flash of light, I caught a glimpse of a man coming towards the car. He approached us and stood beside Damyan's window. He lit a match and peered inside. I saw his brown features, broad flat nose, and shaggy hair. He grinned at Damyan and offered his hand.

"This is Mr. Gar, the American you are to take to Baguio," Goyo told the stranger.

The man nodded. "Good. My name is Ating. You come with me, Mr. Gar."

Damyan took a thin folded slip of paper and handed it to me.

"You give this to the man in Baguio," said Goyo. "His name is Joe Nelson. He is a mestizo who owns the Summer Capital Hotel. He will help you. Do not let anyone else see it."

I took the paper and with the aid of Goyo's knife slit a hole in the lining of my jacket. I slipped the paper inside.

Then I turned to Damyan. "When this is all over, maybe you'll come and play that reed flute for me someday," I said.

Damyan grinned and shook my hand, nodding his head.

"He says, 'Okay'," interpreted Goyo.

I remembered Candy. I asked Goyo to stop by and let her know that I was all right. He did not look too happy about it, but he finally agreed.

"She will get the message," he promised.

"Take care of yourself till I come back," I told him.

I got out of the car and looked at my new friend.

# FOURTEEN

We started our journey in Ating's jeep. It bounced and danced on the road. But in spite of the bouncing, I dozed through most of the trip. Ating woke me up every time we came to a toll station. I forked out money all the way to the mountains.

"Many of the toll stations are closed at night," Ating told me, "because there is no traffic. But some people stay up all night waiting for a chance to make a peso."

I had been away for so many years that the trip was almost like watching the unfolding of an old silent movie. Whenever we came to a settlement we saw rows of nipa houses huddled close together on either side of the road, with the inevitable banana and coconut trees clustered around them. In the villages the roads were cluttered up with dogs, pigs, goats, and chickens. When we approached, Ating sounded his horn sharply. When we were nearly on top of them, the animals rose slowly and meandered to safety. Once a chicken made the mistake of running twice across the road in front of us. There was a loud squawk and thump and then a shower of feathers.

"Got him," said Ating. "We'll have chicken sinigang for breakfast." He backed up the jeep, climbed out and picked up the dead chicken and threw it into the back seat. And we continued on our merry way.

When we reached Bauang we turned off the main road into the mountains.

"We will stop at my house for the rest of the night," said Ating. "The road up the mountains is bad. We will go on at dawn. Have you ever slept in a nipa house?"

"Brother," I told him, "I was born here and I fought in North Africa. I've slept in foxholes."

He laughed.

We pulled up beside a nipa house. I followed Ating towards the bamboo ladder. But I was so stiff and sore I could hardly walk.

"You have been hurt," Ating said.

"I think I have a fractured rib," I said.

"My wife will bandage it for you."

We climbed up the ladder. I had not been inside a nipa house for a long time. Ating swung his flashlight around. The house contained only one big room. The kitchen was separated from the main house by a sawali screen. I caught a glimpse of the little earthen stove that always reminded me of Dutch shoes because of its shape. Five children and Ating's wife were asleep on the floor.

The wife awakened when Ating lit an oil lamp. She scrambled to her feet and came forward, smiling sleepily. She was a short plump women with the good-natured features of the country people. I could see she was expecting another child.

Ating spoke to her in Ilocano. I had forgotten most of that dialect, but I understood that he was telling her about my injuries. She nodded and smiled at me.

"You come to kitchen," she said.

She bathed my cuts, then, from an earthen jug, she took a handful of what looked like mud and spread it on my wounds.

"Tomorrow you healed," she promised, plastering my ribs with the stuff.

I didn't see how mud could heal a fractured rib but it felt cool and soothing. She wound a strip of cloth around my ribs so tightly that I could hardly breathe. It felt good, all right.

"Now you sleep," she said. "I call you for breakfast."

Ating unrolled a mat for me in a far corner of the room and gave me a sheet. I stretched out on it, thinking of the foxholes in Africa. This is luxury, I thought, and fell asleep.

It was still dark when Ating awakened me.

"We eat, then we go," he whispered.

A rooster outside was blowing his lungs out. The other animals under the house were grunting and stirring. I got up, expecting to be stiff. But I was surprised the pain had gone away. Pretty good mud these country people make.

When I had washed the mud off my face, we sat down to eat. Ating's wife must have stayed up all night to prepare breakfast. We had a platter of the inevitable rice, hot and steaming from the fire. The chicken we had killed was now a stew called sinigang. There was fried fish, and in my honor, a fried egg. Ating's wife was upset because they had no silverware.

"Well, I haven't done this in years," I said. "But I learned to eat with my fingers from the Igorots."

The five little Atings were awake. They lined up solemnly around the table to watch the white man eat with his fingers. I was pretty awkward at it and got some rice in my ears. They all burst out laughing. Ating's wife poked me playfully on the shoulder.

"You good man," she laughed. "You like our ways."

I felt like a new man after breakfast. I gave each of the youngsters some coins. I knew Ating's wife would be offended if I offered her money, so I gave her a lighter.

"You have to keep fluid or gasoline in it," I told her.

"That is easy," she said. "My uncle owns a gas station. This is better than electric light and I can take it everywhere with me. You come back again. Next time our oldest daughter sing 'God Bless America' for you."

I patted the oldest daughter's head. "I'll remember that," I told her, "And I'll be back to hear it."

I heard Ating starting the jeep. I went down the ladder while the family gathered in the doorway, waving at me. I had a new heart now. I felt that what I was doing might someday help these people.

Dawn was breaking over the mountains. We skimmed along the road. The country people were already up. Some of them were on the road with baskets and jars on their heads, on their way to the market.

After a while we hit the bad part of the road. I could understand now why Ating refused to drive at night. We came to a sign that read, "Danger. Narrow Roads, Blind Curves, Falling Rocks, Coldest Jail in Luzon."

There was plenty of early morning fog rising out of the

valleys so that it seemed as if we were on the very edge of the world, about to ride off into space. The air grew colder, but our motor grew hotter.

There was plenty of early traffic. The Igorots who were rebuilding the road by hand were already out, hammering rock into gravel and pouring hot tar over new sections of road. Trucks and the first bus from Baguio came roaring past. Sometimes, when we hit a one-way stretch, we had to back up to let them by. It took us two hours and a half to make the twenty miles to the top of the mountain. I thought, several times, that we were going off into space. But somehow Ating kept the jeep on the road, until we finally rounded the last curves. Then I saw ahead the spires of Baguio.

"We stop at Capital Hotel and find out where this fellow Joe Nelson lives," said Ating when we drove into the city.

We pulled up in front of a new building. Ating hopped out of the car and went inside. I climbed out and stood on the curb to stretch my legs.

Baguio is the only American-style city in the Philippines, the only city where the streets and sidewalks are all paved, where no pigs and goats roam loose, and where electricity and running water are available any time.

I could see now that the war had wrought a terrific damage in the city. Most of the big buildings were gutted and ruined. But even at this early hour, I could hear the ring of hammers and saws as the workmen labored to rebuild the city.

I stood on the street looking around. Maybe it was the mountain air that made my spirits light but I felt, suddenly, that I was coming to the end of my hunt. Perhaps in a few minutes I would have solved the mystery of Clem and everything would be all right again.

While I stood there, feeling contented with myself, I saw a figure coming up the streets that jolted me out of my day dreams. It was uncanny the way this guy always popped up at the wrong time, and his arrival was always the forerunner of trouble for me. I would have turned now and run inside the hotel, but it was too late for me. He had already spotted me.

I took a deep breath and tried to act pleased. There was nothing else I could do. Pepe Gonzales walked towards me with a big grin on his face.

# FIFTEEN

Pepe greeted me as if we were brother Shriners meeting at a convention. He pumped my hand, slapped my shoulder and winked knowingly. His first words startled me.

"So, this is how you escape the Montalvos?"

"What?" I cried.

"Estara," laughed Pepe, thumping my chest with his knuckles. "I thought by this time you'd discover she has halitosis."

"She ought to change her toothpaste," I agreed.

I tried to think of some way to get rid of Pepe before Ating came out of the hotel. But I was expecting snow in Manila. His clutch on my arm told me he was there for the duration.

"What brought you to Baguio?" I asked.

"Oh, we always come up at this time of year," he answered. "It's too hot in Manila." He lit a cigarette. "I suppose you came up to look over your mine?"

I decided to let Pepe know where I stood. Maybe he would stop playing cops and robber with me.

"It won't do me any good to look at the mine," I said. "I haven't got the money to reopen it."

"Undoubtedly you could get someone to finance it," said Pepe. "A banker, perhaps."

"I turned down one offer," I told him. "I didn't like the terms of the loan."

I was a little surprised at Pepe's reaction. He seemed genuinely amused.

"What was wrong?" he asked. "Halitosis?"

"Yes," I said. "It smelled pretty bad."

"There are many ways to catch a duck," said Pepe.

I saw Ating come out of the hotel. He saw me talking to Pepe. He passed us on the sidewalk without looking at me, and climbed into his jeep.

"Suppose we have some coffee," suggested Pepe.

"Not now, thanks," I said. "I want to go up the hill and look at my old summer home. I don't know yet how badly it was damaged."

It was the wrong thing to say. Pepe nodded.

"I'll go with you," he said. "Do you have a car?"

I shook my head. He looked up and down the street. Then his eyes fell on Ating. He approached the jeep.

"Would you like to make a couple of pesos?" he asked.

Ating looked at him sullenly.

"I'm not a taxi," he said.

"Of course not," agreed Pepe. "I just thought you might like to earn a couple of pesos."

"I'll do it for five," said Ating suddenly.

"Three-fifty," said Ating.

"It's a deal," said Pepe. He opened the door and pushed me inside. "That's what I love about this country," he commented. "It's easy to do business."

I gave Ating the direction and sat back to look at the countryside. The fighting must have been hell. I saw hundreds of ruined pines. Everywhere, even down into the heart of town, were the ugly little makeshift huts, the barong-barongs erected by the squatters. When we reached my house, I sat looking at it for a minute in silence.

The house was still standing and the front door seemed intact. But the windows were all broken and the steps leading up to the porch were gone.

"I wonder what happened to the stairs," I said. "There's no sign of them."

"Oh, the squatters probably carried them away," said Pepe. "After the fighting was over they carried away everything they could move." He pointed to a bamboo ladder on the ground. "Somebody must be living in your house."

We leaned the ladder against the porch and climbed up. The door was locked or bolted inside. I pounded on the door and finally a dark face appeared in one of the broken windows.

"I am the owner of this house," I said. "Open the door, please."

The face disappeared. I heard voices inside, then a patter of bare feet.

The door opened and we walked into the wide hall.

An Igorot and his wife and three youngsters stared at us.

"I am the caretaker," said the man.

"Thanks for taking care of the house," I said.

He grunted. I looked around.

It was impossible to go to the second floor. The upper half of the staircase was completely wrecked. There was not a stick of furniture in sight. I walked into the room on the right which had formerly been a bedroom. The windows had all been boarded up; gray light filtered through the cracks. The room was bare. Even the light fixtures had been torn out.

I opened the door that led to the adjoining bath and found myself staring at another family who were apparently living in the bathroom. They had erected a charcoal stove in the porcelain bathtub. The walls were black with soot. The family squatted around on the floor, grinning at me.

I felt sick. I turned away.

The rest of the house was just as bad. In another bathroom, I found that all the fixtures had been taken away. When we reached the kitchen, I wondered why the self-styled caretakers bothered to lock the front door. There was a hole in the wall big enough to drive an automobile through.

I went to the terrace that had once been the envy of our friends and stared across the woodland. I wasn't looking at the pine trees, though. I was seeing our house in the gay years when I had been a boy and Mother and Dad had been alive and Clem and Candy would come to visit us. Now everything was changed and my magic world was gone.

I almost forgot why I had come to Baguio until I thought of Clem. And then I remembered that I was trying to find him and that I had to see a fellow named Joe Nelson.

I swung around. Pepe was eyeing me sympathetically.

"I have to get back to town," I said.

"Of course," said Pepe quietly. He fell into step beside

me as we walked back through the empty house. "Where are you staying?"

"At the Summer Capital Hotel," I said, trying to forestall any invitation from him.

"Oh, that's Joe Nelson's hotel," said Pepe. "Too bad about Joe, wasn't it?"

A grim misgiving took hold of me. I stood where I was while I stared at Pepe.

"What do you mean?" I asked.

"Why, didn't you hear the news?" asked Pepe. "Joe was found dead this morning."

# SIXTEEN

Joe Nelson dead. I was stunned. If I had arrived a few hours sooner I might have saved his life. Now my only possible lead to Clem was gone. There was no doubt in my mind that Nelson was murdered. Three deaths because of me. Somebody was trying awfully hard to keep me from finding Clem.

"How did Joe Nelson die?" I asked.

"He had an accident," said Pepe. "A very peculiar accident. It seems he was out for a walk in the moonlight and went too close to the edge of a cliff. If it had been anyone else, we would have thought he was drunk. But Joe did not drink."

Pepe started down the bamboo ladder. I followed him.

"Could Joe have been pushed?"

Pepe reached the ground and stood looking up at me. For the second time since I knew him I notice how cold his eyes could be.

"The police said it was accidental," answered Pepe. "And who can dispute the word of the police?"

We walked slowly to the jeep. There was a fine touch of irony in Pepe's last remark. Everybody knows that the police here are grossly underpaid and that almost anyone on the force would sell his grandmother for fifty centavos.

Ating started the motor and we rode back to the city.

"A man in this country doesn't know his enemies any more," I commented.

"Sometimes," said Pepe softly, "a man doesn't recognize his friends either."

I glanced sharply at him, trying to fathom his meaning. It

94

was funny. He had used almost the same words as Rosa Linkhow when I visited her at Linda Mujer. What happened here, anyway? It hadn't always been like this. Before the war we knew our friends. We trusted one another. Now it was changed. Somehow, everyone now seemed pitiful to me. Everyone was looking for someone to trust. And nobody could find it. Even Pepe.

His words were an invitation to confide my troubles to him. And it is true, I might have done it were it not for the fact that I had seen Pepe and Rosa at that off-the-record meeting and had seen Rosa give him that mysterious slip of paper. It meant that Pepe was lined up with the Montalvo crowd. It meant that we could never be friends. I was sorry. Under different circumstances, I could have had a deep liking for him.

I had to get rid of Pepe. I had been delayed too many times and something told me that time was running short. I had to go out on my own now. Alone, I had to find the Igorot who could take me to Clem.

"Where can we drop you?" I asked Pepe.

"I'm staying at the Zigzag Hotel," he said.

We were back in the city. When we left the car in front of the hotel, Pepe paused for a minute and leaned his head inside the jeep. Whatever emotion had bothered him a few minutes before was gone. He was himself again, full of grins and twinkles.

"There's good hunting in the mountains," said Pepe. "We must go together soon."

"We must," I promised.

I watched him enter the hotel. Then we pulled away from the curb.

"It looks like I'll have to look alone for Damyan's friend," I told Ating.

"Who was that man?" Ating asked.

"His name is Pepe Gonzales," I said. "I think he is dangerous."

"I think he killed Joe Nelson," said Ating. "If I find out for sure—"

"Take it easy for a while," I advised him. "I have to find a man and I don't even know his name."

"I take you to the market place now," said Ating. "That's the best place to look for an Igorot."

My chin was beginning to feel scratchy. I had not shaved in two days and I knew that I must be a sight fit to scare even an Igorot. I told Ating to drop me at the drugstore, and that I would check in at the Summer Capital Hotel for a quick cleanup.

"I'll find you in about half an hour at the market," I told him.

I bought a toothbrush and paste and soap and a razor at the drugstore and then walked up the hill to the hotel.

"Give me a room with a shower," I told the clerk.

He studied his list a long time. Finally he said, "I can give you a room with a bath that has a tub, or I can give you a room with a bath that has a shower. The shower does not work. Which would you prefer, sir?"

"Give me the one that works," I said.

He charged me fifteen pesos—seven-fifty American money —for a cubbyhole overlooking the street. The bed was an iron cot without a spread and the door had no key. But it had a bath with all the fixings. Except hot water.

But even cold water felt good. I splashed around and enjoyed the clean smell of soap on my skin. I shaved and dressed. I examined my eye and mouth that Bruiser and Killer had punished so ruthlessly. The swelling in my eye had almost disappeared and my cut lips were healing. I stood before the mirror, marveling over the homemade medication that Ating's wife had applied on me.

Then I heard footsteps coming down the hall. The footsteps stopped outside the door. There was a knock.

I thought my visitor was Ating, so I called out, "Come in. There's no key."

The door opened. I groaned when I saw Pepe.

He wasn't grinning now. He entered quickly and shut the door and leaned against it.

"You should not have registered here under your own name," said Pepe. "It makes you easy to find."

I stared at him. "What do you mean?"

"I came to tell you that some friends of yours are in town. They are looking for you. Look out the window."

I swung around and went to the window. Across the street I saw Montalvo's familiar black car. Killer was at the wheel. As I watched, Bruiser climbed out of the front seat and started across the street towards my hotel.

"Let's get out through the back door," said Pepe.

I stuck my razor and toothbrush in my pocket and followed him down the hall. We hurried down a flight of steps that led to a rear entrance. As we went down the steps, I heard the front door open and slam. I sprinted after Pepe. We ran to a rear balcony and down another flight of stone stairs into a narrow parking lot. At one end of the lot was the rubble of a destroyed wall. We climbed up the debris and dropped on the other side.

We were in an alley that led uphill past rows of makeshift shacks. We were both breathing hard when we reached the top. We came out on another street and, with grim humor, I noticed that we were in front of the police station.

"Maybe this would be a good place to stay," I said.

Pepe shook his head and took my arm.

"Better go down to the market place."

"Why are you doing this for me?" I asked.

He flashed me two rows of pearly white teeth.

"I'd be sorry to see you marry Estara," he said. Then he added, "Maybe I like you."

He was a hard guy to make out. He had just saved my life. Maybe he had only acted on impulse. But the fact remained that he would not lay his cards on the table and I could not trust him very far.

The market is the best hiding place in Baguio. The midday crowds were milling around the open stalls. Every kind of product was on display, from new suits to fresh fish and strawberries. I was hoping to shake Pepe off. Pepe, however, kept hard on my heels. But I finally lost sight of him and stepped before a counter piled high with hand-carved wooden slippers.

Then I saw Ating coming towards me. He had a squat Igorot in tow. The newcomer was typical Igorot. He wore a Navy jacket that almost hit his knees, but no pants. His hair was long and held back by a headband.

"I found our friend," said Ating.

The Igorot nodded briefly at me and led us out through the back to a narrow street that was crowded with parked produce trucks. He halted beside one of the trucks and turned to me.

"You have a ring?" he asked.

I took the bronze ring out of my pocket and showed it to him. He turned it over and over in his hand, studying the workmanship. Finally, he nodded his head.

"This was made in Baung-baung, a village next to mine, in the Kalinga country," he said.

I dug inside the lining of my jacket for the slip of paper that Damyan had given me. The Igorot shook his head at the paper.

"I will take you to the village of Bacnutan, which is my home. You will show this paper to our chief."

I turned to Ating and held out my hand.

"Inyan will take care of you," said Ating.

I thanked Ating for all his trouble. I offered him money, but he refused. Strange people, unlike the ones in Manila.

Ating waved goodbye when we started off. As we pulled out of the market place, I saw Pepe standing in front of a vegetable stand. He was looking up and down the street. I drew back. His eyes suddenly fell on Inyan when we drove past him. I felt certain that he did not see me. Anyway, the last place where he would look for me would be in a truck of cabbages.

# SEVENTEEN

We drove slowly over the uneven road and through the famous Trinidad Valley from which come most of the cultivated vegetables and fruits that supply Baguio and Manila. There was very little traffic now. The empty trucks would be returning from the market at sundown.

"How far will we travel in this truck?" I asked Inyan.

"We go about ten kilometers beyond the American gas station," he said. "Then we leave the truck and go on foot down the mountains to the Kalinga country."

I remembered the American gas station from years gone by. It was owned by an American who had settled there after the Spanish War and had married an Igorot woman and raised a flock of little Igorots. Because of the site of his gas station, everybody called him Mr. Mountain. I had never learned his real name.

"Is Mr. Mountain still alive?" I asked.

Inyan's face relaxed. He nodded several times.

"Still alive. He's an old man now. Lots of grandchildren."

Our conversation waned after that. Igorots are economical with words. They don't go in for small talk or the dissimulations that are considered necessary in polite society. Strange people. They only believe in saying what they mean.

I lit a cigarette and looked around at the scenery, beyond the cultivated plains to the wall of mountains that surrounded us. They were bearded with thick green foliage and the promontories were mantled in blue. The air was growing thinner and cooler as we climbed. I began to wish I had a Navy jacket like Inyan, but why his bare legs did not freeze was a mystery to me.

We left the valley and began chugging up a winding mountain road. I saw Inyan glance into the mirror over the windshield and frown slightly. Then I saw a jeep come into view from around a curve.

We had already left the densely inhabited canyons. There were now only a few grass houses perched here and there like birds' nests on the mountainside. Inyan stepped on the accelerator, but the road had many sudden dips and sharp curves.

I glanced through the back window again. The jeep was coming closer. Then it maintained a steady pace behind us. But I could not identify the passengers.

"Are there any other settlements along this road?" I asked.

"Only at Mr. Mountain's gas station," said Inyan.

"Maybe the jeep is heading that way," I said.

Inyan grunted and gained speed when we came to a downhill stretch. We were at a disadvantage for speed, however. The jeep could easily have passed us by, but it just tagged along behind. I began to wonder if the Montalvo gang had traced us. Then I saw the white painted wooden building of the American gas station.

"We better stop at Mr. Mountain's," said Inyan. "If the jeep is after us we'll have help there."

I nodded.

We pulled up at the gas station. The radiator was boiling. The jeep came rolling behind us and stopped across the road. Then I saw Pepe jump out. The jeep swung around and headed back towards Baguio. Pepe stood in the road, waving his arm. He started towards us.

"Who's that?" asked Inyan.

"That's a guy who has been chasing me all over the Philippines," I said. "I don't know exactly what he's up to, but I don't want him on this trip."

Pepe was beside the truck now, grinning impishly.

"Since I've come this far," he greeted us, "you may as well take me with you. Are you going hunting?"

"Yes, I'm going hunting," I said. "You may find this a rugged trip before you're through."

"Oh, I'm not as soft as you think," said Pepe.

While we waited for the engine to cool, we walked to

stretch our legs. We bought a bunch of bananas at the little stand that adjoined the gas station and quenched our thirst with the milk of young coconuts. But I didn't see any sign of Mr. Mountain.

It was late in the afternoon now. We piled into the truck and continued our journey.

"We will spend the night with friends in the mountains," said Inyan. "Tomorrow we go down into the valley."

It was nearly sunset when we reached the end of the road. Inyan parked the truck off the road and locked it. Pepe and I stood in silence on the edge of the mountain looking down a wide valley.

Far down in the blue haze that stretched below us was the country that belonged to the Kalinga tribe. No one can enter this territory without a guide. It is well guarded by watchful Kalinga warriors who are noted for their distrust of strangers and their deadly accuracy with poisoned spears. Long ago Dad and Clem and I had gone down there a few times on hunting trips. It was somewhere down there that I had bought the bronze ring for Clem. And now the ring was leading me back.

Inyan joined us and took the lead. He started down the side of the mountain, moving sideways instead of forward. There may have been a trail, but it was invisible, except to an Igorot. I followed behind Inyan, and Pepe trailed after us. Pepe and I moved slowly and cautiously, following Inyan's tracks carefully. Going down a mountainside isn't too hard, and the Igorots seem to have solved the problem by climbing sideways. I've seen them climb whole mountain slopes in this fashion with heavy baskets on their heads, moving quickly and never getting out of breath.

Sunset was full upon us now. The sky was bloody red. It would be pitch dark in a minute. There is no twilight in the mountains.

"Is it far to the house of your friends?" I called to Inyan.

He glanced up at me and shook his head.

"Not far," he said. "We get there by dark."

Long shadows crept ahead of us. I glanced up once to see how Pepe was making it. I could see his face in the waning light, suddenly serious and determined as he studied his descent.

"I should have brought a flashlight," he said.

"We'll be there soon," Inyan shouted back.

I paused and looked down over bushes and trees. About a hundred yards below, I saw the roof of a grass house. I turned around to tell Pepe. And then I saw him slip.

His foot skidded on a rock and he came crashing towards me. I reached out to grab him and the force of the impact hurled us both smashing against a young tree.

He landed on top of me. I was senseless for a moment. Then Pepe slowly crawled to his feet. There was a long scratch across his check. He looked down at me.

"That was a close call. Are you all right?"

I sat up. There was a shooting pain in my side. My fractured rib was probably loose again. I crawled to my feet and found I could not put my weight on my left foot.

"I think I broke a leg," I said.

Inyan came back to us. He put one of my arms around his shoulder and told me to put the other one around Pepe. We started downwards again.

"It looks as if you'll be laid up for a few days," said Pepe.

Something in his tone arrested me. I looked at him from the corner of my eye. In the gray light his expression was blurred. But it seemed that there was a little smirk of satisfaction around the lines of his mouth.

It began to dawn on me that his fall had not been accidental. As we moved slowly downward towards the little grass house, I wondered what his next move would be.

Then we saw a couple of naked brown children running towards us. They stopped when they spotted Pepe and me. Inyan spoke to them in their dialect and they turned and ran back to the house.

The father came out and approached us, dressed in the traditional loincloth. He was a tall and broad-shouldered Igorot who was very handsome until he opened his mouth. He was one of the old-fashioned Igorots who had filed his teeth and painted them black.

Inyan talked to him in their own tongue, then introduced Pepe and me. The man greeted us courteously in English and welcomed us to his home. He and Inyan made a chair of their hands and carried me the rest of the way.

Their house was the usual one-room affair without furniture. The wife seemed a little startled when she saw us, but she smiled shyly and invited us inside. The house was full of half a dozen more naked youngsters of various ages, who clustered together in a corner, peering at us curiously.

They put me on the floor and propped me up with a wooden pillow. Inyan set my leg together, and the woman bound it tightly with splints.

"Your leg not broken," pronounced Inyan, "You stay off it tomorrow. By the next day you walk again."

I fervently hoped so. Now that my chase was drawing to a close, I felt it was imperative that I get to the Kalinga village without more delay. Something kept telling me that if I didn't get there soon it would be too late. And I was worried about where Pepe fitted into the picture.

Pepe, however, had changed roles. Instead of the smart young man-about-town, he was having fun being One of The People. He squatted on the floor and told native jokes and acted them out, and even made the woman laugh. When dinner, consisting of stewed wild game and rice and sweet potatoes, was served, he sat down and ate with his fingers as if he had always done so. The woman and her children watched us from the background. They were amused when Pepe and I dipped our fingers in the common earthen pot. Pepe looked over at me once and winked. His chin was greasy.

"There's more flavor when you eat this way," he told me. "If I ever become President I'll pass a law doing away with silverware. The politicians will all die of starvation and I'll be known as the savior of my country."

I laughed. It was impossible to dislike Pepe. And if I only felt sure of him, I could have enjoyed his company.

When bedtime came we all stretched on the floor, our heads supported by wooden pillows. The thought flashed through my mind that maybe Pepe planned to knife us all while we slept. Then I dismissed the idea. If he had wanted to kill me he could have done it several times before without going to all this trouble.

I noticed, however, that Inyan did not lie down with the rest of us. He sat with his back to the door, puffing his cigar. I turned towards the wall, hoping for sleep. If Inyan was going to act as my watchdog, I would not have to worry. I fell asleep.

Sleep is peace. I'm in favor of more of it. Maybe that would end war. Maybe that's what the United Nations need instead of speeches. Anyway, I enjoyed it so much that when someone touched me on the shoulder, I opened my eyes with a start.

Daylight was streaming through the window. Inyan was leaning over me.

"You don't have to worry about your friend any more," he said. "He's gone."

"What?"

"He left in the middle of the night," said Inyan. "I moved away from the door and sat in another corner and saw him go."

"Perhaps he went back to Baguio," said Inyan. "If he tried to travel alone into the Kalinga country, especially at night, he is probably dead by now."

I leaned back on my elbow to think it over. I could not understand why Pepe would suddenly leave us, after being so hot on my trail.

And then I discovered that my bronze ring was missing.

# EIGHTEEN

At first I thought the bronze ring might have rolled out of my pocket when Pepe and I fell on the mountainside. But I recalled that I had felt it in my pocket before I went to sleep. Inyan and I searched the floor. No luck. The ring was gone.

I was sure then that Pepe had taken the ring from me before he slipped away in the night. It increased my urgency to get going, and I smarted with impatience over the delay that my injured leg was causing. The hunt was resolving into a race, a race against time. And if Pepe had the ring it would not be hard for him to persuade someone to guide him across the Kalinga country. I was convinced now that the ring was mixed up with the conspiracy of the Manila collaborators, and that if Clem were still alive he had the solution to the mystery.

I forced myself to lay quietly on my back to give my leg a chance to heal. Reaction from the accident set in and made me drowsy and I dozed most of the day. But by evening I was up again, hobbling painfully around the small house. I was determined to push on the next day.

So at dawn we set out. Our host accompanied us part of the way.

The valley below us still slept in a blue mist. Over in the east pale yellow fingers of light edged over the rim of the mountains. The foliage and tall grass bent with heavy dew, and we became wet with the tingling coolness.

We reached the floor of the valley at noon. Here our host told us goodbye. The heat now was intense after the coolness of the high altitude. When we came to a running stream I threw myself down on my stomach and drank dog-style from the brook. Then I cooled my head and face in the limpid water.

Across the stream a meadow of wild grasses grew waist-high and beyond it was a forest. I wetted my handkerchief and tied it around my forehead before we cross the stream. By the time we had gone a quarter of a mile, the handkerchief was stiff and dry from the heat. The plain stretched out before us, widening as we walked, like an elastic band, while the forest kept receding from us.

I noticed that Inyan was looking around and studying the ground.

"Looking for snakes?" I asked.

He shook his head.

"I'm trying to see if your friend passed this way," he said. "I cannot find any trace of him."

"Maybe a wild animal got him," I said.

He shrugged. "Maybe. But sounds carry great distances at night and I heard no cries."

Little by little we seemed to be gaining on the forest. It was a good thing. My head was beginning to spin and it seemed to me that the air was suddenly full of bright flashes of red and green and yellow and purple, sharp little pinpoints of color that jumped and poked at my eyeballs.

Then Inyan touched me on the arm. He stood rigid like a bird dog, staring towards the forest. I stood beside him. I screwed up my eyes as I peered ahead, trying to make out what had caught his attention. All I could see was the green curtain of the forest. Then he emitted a high weird whistle that reminded me of the cry of a wild bird.

From the forest came an answering call. The whistles were exchanged back and forth a few times. Inyan moved forward again. I followed him. As we approached the forest, I saw several figures emerge from behind the trees.

They were big fellows, their coppery bodies naked except for loincloths, their long, wild-looking hair held back by headbands. They carried black spears.

I thought, Oh, Jehosephat, where are my Boy Scout tricks? But all I could remember was how to build a fire, and these fellows didn't look as if they needed a fire to set them going.

Inyan motioned me to wait. I didn't argue. I watched him go forward. Then he was talking to the hunters. They glared in my direction. Maybe because I was a sissy and wore pants. Finally, I saw them rest their spears on the ground. Inyan motioned me to come join the party. I was relieved.

"They will accompany us to my village," said Inyan. "They are my people."

"Have they seen Pepe?" I asked.

"They say no one else has come this way."

We followed them into the thick gloom of the forest. The trees grew so close together that only dapples of light penetrated through the branches. One of the warriors led the way. The others fell in behind us. All the leader needed was a pair of khaki pants and I could imagine him barking. "Hep, two, three, four!"

The forest was silent. Not even a breath of air rustled the leaves of the trees. Even the myriads of small bugs that circled our heads seemed too listless to buzz. They merely dug their little stingers into me, sucking my blood, until after an hour my arms and legs looked as if I had been giving transfusions. It seems to be only the white people who suffer from bug bites in the tropics. The natives say it is because of the way we smell.

Once we came upon a horde of small monkeys. Their screams shattered the silence of the forest. Then they disappeared, scattering in all directions, and everything was still again.

At sundown we came to a clearing. Inyan said we would make our camp for the night. The young men disappeared again into the forest. I was so exhausted that I sank down and sat leaning against the nearest tree. Inyan gathered wood and built a fire. Through a haze of half-consciousness, I inhaled the pungent smoke. I remembered the trip that Dad and Clem and I had made years before. Clem and I had pretended we were Igorot hunters and had gone out to trap birds and had only succeeded in catching a small monkey.

In a little while the young men returned. They had better luck than Clem and me. Some of them caught wild game. Inyan roasted the birds and one of the hunters cut young bamboo shoots for our drinking water.

We took turns keeping watch. As soon as it was dark the

forest came awake. All night long there were mysterious rustles and movements, sudden sharp cries and eerie calls of the forest creatures, followed by abrupt silence that was more uncanny than the noise. We kept the fire going so that none of the animals would venture near us. Once I awoke with a start and saw four eyes glowing at me from across the fire. Then the animals turned and went away. I had a quick glimpse of two long black bodies slinking into the darkness.

As soon as it was light we were up again. We finished what was left of the food and continued our journey.

I was sure now that Pepe could not make this trip alone. But I was uneasy and impatient to get to Inyan's village. I had to admit that Pepe had outsmarted me on almost every count and I wouldn't have been surprised to reach the village and find out that he had arrived by parachute.

Late in the afternoon we emerged from the forest and found ourselves on a mesa overlooking a valley. Spread out before us I could see uneven rows of what looked like enormous mushrooms.

"There is my village," said Inyan.

News of our coming must have reached the village ahead of us, because when we arrived the whole population seemed to have turned out to greet us. Instinctively I looked around to see if Pepe was on the welcoming committee. I half-expected to see him dash out from among the crowd, pump my hand and tell me the convention hall was on my right. There was no sight of him, however.

The mushrooms had resolved themselves into little grass houses. The villagers were lined up on one side of the road. The women were dressed in sarongs. Some of them wore gold and silver bands around their legs and arms. There was no distrust here, such as the hunters in the forest had displayed. There was only open curiosity.

Inyan took me to the house of the chief. He was squatting under a tree in front of his house and carving what looked like a man's head out of a piece of wood. I was surprised to find that the chief was only a young man. He was big and well built, with a pair of shoulders like a quarterback. He would have been handsome if his teeth had not been stained black.

Inyan told him who I was and that I had been sent to him by Damyan. The chief turned to me and did a surprising thing for an Igorot. He smiled and held out his hand. Then he welcomed me in the most cultured American accent I had ever heard west of New York.

"My father knew your father, Mr. Stanley," he said. "You came to our valley to hunt a long time age." He let my hand go. "We are almost brothers, you know," he continued. "I attended Columbia, too. But I was back before the war started."

Well, it was a small world. Or maybe it was only a small valley. I had forgotten that the Kalinga tribe were the best educated of the Igorots. It is their tradition that no matter where their chief chooses to live he always spends one month a year with his people.

I felt at ease with him. It was almost like running into a fraternity brother in the middle of Africa. We squatted on the ground, or rather, he squatted while I sat with my knees propped under my chin. I related my troubles and showed him the letter that Damyan had given me. I told him about the loss of the bronze ring.

He read the letter, nodding his head.

"The man you are looking for has never been here," he said. "But I am told that in the village of Baung-Baung there is a white man who was a leader of the guerillas during the war. He was badly injured and he was taken there for safety. He was lived there ever since. His name is Mayo."

I sighed with relief. So, Clem was still alive.

"He is my oldest friend," I said. "He is the man I'm looking for. How far is Baung-Baung?"

"About a day's journey from here," smiled the chief. "But you can't possibly leave before morning. It is a hard trip into mountainous country and you look tired."

I nodded in weary agreement. He turned his head and called to someone. A woman came out of the house with a cup which she presented to me.

"Tapuey," said the chief. "Perhaps you remember it."

I remembered hearing my father hiccuping after a tapuey session. He had said it was a little milder than pure alcohol and a little stronger than brandy. I tasted the stuff and decided the old man had been a pretty good judge of liquor. There was a hint of sweetness in the flavor, but most of that was lost in the fiery sensation when the liquid scalded my throat. I swallowed the rest in one gulp and in half a minute felt equal to taking on Montalvo, Bruiser, and Killer, all in one thrust.

The chief smiled. He said, "After you have a swim in the river, you will feel like joining the dance tonight."

A swim was just what I wanted. The woman reappeared and led me beyond the house to a small river. I stripped off my clothes and slipped into the cool flowing water and wallowed around like a carabao. I decided that Manila had nothing to offer that these people didn't have. There was no problem of running water, the liquor was plentiful and potent, and nobody lurked in doorways waiting to beat you over the head. And I was glad that I was going to stay and see the floor show.

When I came out of the water the air was still warm enough to dry me. I dressed and returned to the chief's house. It was now growing dark. A great bonfire was blazing in front of the house and the air was tangy with the aroma of roasting pig.

The chief led me to a place around the bonfire to a group of elderly men. He introduced me to them and told me they were the elders of the village. An enormous cup of tapuey was pushed into my hands. I was about to drink it down when I remembered my father's hiccups. So I sipped a little and passed the cup to the next man. Everybody was smoking clay pipes, and I was given one. The tobacco was the raw undiluted variety. But nobody seemed to be concerned about cigarette cough. After a few puffs we dipped into the tapuey again. It became a pleasant circle of movement—tapuey and pipe, like pretzels and beer. After a while, as the fumes of tapuey and tobacco merged pleasantly in my head, I decided it would be a good idea to start my own Igorot village, and I said so. The chief thought that was funny. And then dinner was announced.

After dinner the young people danced for us. The musicians thumped on hollow wooden drums and blew on reed flutes with their noses. The young people did not dance Western-fashion, but in long lines facing each other. There was more tapuey and a lot of talk. I leaned contentedly against a tree and decided that there was no great hurry to go to Baung-Baung. I felt relaxed and cozy and decided it would be pleasant to sit just where I was for a few years. I closed my eyes to think it over.

When I opened my eyes again sunlight was streaming across the sky and the chief was standing beside me.

"You will want to start early on your trip," he said. "Inyan will accompany you and I will send you an escort."

He gave me back the letter Damyan had given me and told me to give it to the chief at Baung-Baung. He also sent gifts to the chief. After a hurried breakfast we shook hands and parted.

After leaving Bacnutan we traveled across the grassy floor of the valley most of the morning, then at noon began a steep ascent into the mountains. It was midafternoon when we reached Baung-Baung.

When we entered the village I knew at once something was wrong. No one was in sight to greet us. We walked past long rows of grass houses. I had the feeling of many eyes staring and watching us, but whenever I looked around, no one was in view. We stopped before the house of the chief and Inyan climbed up to the door.

An old man with a body as withered as a dried cigar appeared. He and Inyan talked together, then Inyan presented him the gifts from the other chief. Finally, the old chief came down the steps towards me. He saluted me gravely, but there was something guarded in his manner that made me uneasy. I glanced again towards the deserted road of the village, and once more I was conscious of the scrutiny of dozens of eyes peering at me from darkened doorways.

"Will you come into my house?" asked the chief.

I looked towards his house, from which there was no movement of life, and again I was assailed by uneasiness. I decided to stay where I was until I saw his reaction to my story. So I told him at once about the bronze ring and Clem, and showed him Damyan's letter.

He read the letter through. He looked at me silently. Then his thin voice broke the stillness, and his first words explained the terror that had seized the village. "It is too bad you did not arrive sooner," said the chief. "The white man was murdered two days ago."

# NINETEEN

I stared at the old chief in shocked silence.

"Clem Mayo – murdered?" I repeated.

"Yes," said the chief.

He must have caught the bleakness of my feeling because he motioned me to follow him into the house. We sat on the floor in the cool darkness, and somebody shoved a small cup of tapuey in my hand. The fiery liquor did not mitigate my sense of loss; rather it served to sharpen it. It was several minutes before I could bring myself to talk.

"How did he die?" I asked.

And then the reason for chief's uneasiness became apparent. He hesitated almost a minute before he answered. When he spoke his voice was dry, like a piece of rotting wood.

"The shame is on our village," said the old man. "The white man was stabbed by one of our own hunters."

His feeling of self-indictment was so sincere that I could not bring myself to blame him personally. I know the sense of honor among these people and that the acts of any member of their tribe affect them all.

"Tell me about it," I said.

The chief picked up his pipe. One of the women of his household brought another pipe for me. She lighted the bowls for us and we puffed in silence for a few minutes. Then the chief began his story.

"During the war the white man was a leader among the guerillas. Many of his followers were from our people. He was brave and earned our respect. One night, he went out alone to meet a commando from America. He waited long past the appointed time. Finally, he saw a man coming towards him. When Mr. Mayo advanced, the newcomer shot him. Much later, his young daughter Tampa came running into our camp. She told us that through treachery the commando had been betrayed and that it was one of the enemy who had shot her father. We went out to look for Mr. Mayo."

Thus far the chief's story dovetailed with the story Candy had told me. Of course, she would have had no way of knowing about the betrayal. I waited for the old chief to suck on his pipe before he continued.

"Mr. Mayo was alive when we found him," said the old man. "But he was badly wounded. We brought him here to our village and nursed him. But he was never able to walk again. When peace came he continued to live among us."

"Didn't he ever mention his wife or express a desire to see her?" I interrupted.

The chief shook his head. "We believed that his injury had affected his memory. He would sit in silence for days, as if trying to recall something."

"Amnesia?"

"Perhaps," said the chief. He went on with his story. "Not long ago we learned from Damyan of Manila that the Americans were putting on trial those who had betrayed us during the war. Mr. Mayo sent his bronze ring to Manila in the hope that someone of the underground would see it and come to him. Mr. Mayo wrote a letter addressed to his friend Stanley, and whoever came from the underground was to take the letter and deliver it. Mr. Mayo gave me the letter to hold for the right man. He seemed to know that death was waiting for him."

Something like the rustle of dry wind through the grass passed from the chief's lips.

"Two nights ago, one of our men killed Mr. Mayo. We caught him. The murderer had no personal enmity for the white man, but we found much money that he had hidden in his house. When the other white man came to our village yesterday, he told us to turn the murderer over to the police in Baguio. We agreed to do this, and some of our warriors went with him last night in the company of the other white man."

"What other white man?"

The old chief looked at me with surprise.

"Mr. Mayo's friend, Gar Stanley, of course. He came to our village yesterday and showed me the bronze ring."

I groaned. I should have known it. I should have known that Pepe had beat me to the punch again. How he had made the trip, I could not imagine. But the important thing was that he had reached the village ahead of me.

"What about the letter?" I asked.

"I gave the letter to Mr. Stanley," said the chief. "He was grieved over Mr. Mayo's death, but the letter seemed to please him."

The shock of Clem's violent death, together with the loss of the letter, threw me into a mental nosedive. I had failed in everything. I had been unable to save Clem's life. I had failed to help him in any way. Everything I had attempted had turned out to be a fumble. Then I thought of Tampa.

"What about the girl, Tampa?" I asked.

"After her father's death we sent her to work in the gold mine that has just reopened. We did this for her own safety and because she did not want to marry any of our young men."

"Did you tell Pepe – the other white man, I mean, about Tampa?"

The chief shook his head.

"She is only a woman," he said. "She does not enter into this affair."

I asked the chief how I could get to the mine.

"There is a road not far from our village," he said, "which leads directly there. I own a jeep," he added. "I will tell my man to drive you."

I stood up. "I would like to leave at once."

Ordinarily the chief would have been offended if I refused to stay overnight. But the village was at this time so wrapped up in its trouble over Clem's death that I think the old chief was relieved when he knew I was leaving.

He insisted, however, that I stay long enough to eat. We had wild fowl and rice and sweet potatoes, washed down with tapuey. But the food seemed tasteless, and I wanted to be on my way.

Before I left the chief took me to the tree where Clem had been cremated. I knew their custom of tying the dead to a tree before burying it. I looked at the blackened stump and I could not keep back the mist that came to my eyes. I thought of poor Clem, living his last years as a paralytic. I realized, too, that the war had affected his mind. Maybe he was better off this way.

I joined Inyan and the other men who were to take me to the mine.

It was now dark. We set off in single file, marching into the mountains, carrying blazing torches to light our way. We must have made a weird procession. Some of the men had brought their flutes and made the deep sad music that no other flute players in the world can imitate.

It was late in the night when we reached the spot where the chief's jeep was hidden. Inyan and another man and I climbed into the jeep. The others stood around while we started the motor. The ruddy glow from the torches highlighted their cheekbones and firm jaws. I thanked them. They grunted amicably. Then we started off.

We drove for a while over bumpy terrain that no machine but a jeep could have maneuvered. Then we hit the road and it was smooth sailing. I looked back. All I could see was the procession of bobbing torches going back to their village.

We reached the gold mine shortly after dawn.

We drove down the narrow road built into the mountainside and pulled up before the heavy gates. The guards had just changed.

Workers were moving inside the long rows of wooden huts. Each building was long enough to house a dozen separate families. Dark women and children appeared at the windows.

I told the guards what we wanted. They conferred among themselves for a few minutes. Then one of them went inside the guard depot and came back with his chief.

"What do you want?" he barked.

"I want to see the girl, Tampa, from Baung-Baung."

"You can't come in here," he said.

"I only want to see Tampa," I insisted.

"You can't take her away."

I began to get mad.

"You can't keep her here," I said. "She is an American citizen. If you don't let me see her, I'll come back here with the chief of police. Bring me the superintendent."

He swung on his heel and returned to the depot. I could not figure out the reason for this attitude. The workers were not kept as slave labor. They were all free to come and go as they pleased.

While I was debating whether to crash the gate or not, a tall Filipino dressed in khaki shirt and trousers came out of the depot.

"I am the assistant superintendent," he told me. "What is it you want?"

I explained that I wanted to see Tampa. He shook his head.

"There is no such person here," he said.

I climbed out of the jeep and walked up to the gate.

"If you don't let me talk to the girl," I said, "I'll have the American Consul on your neck."

He shrugged. "We have no wish to detain an American. I'll help you look through all the workers' houses. If, as you insist, the girl is here, she is free to go with you, if that is her wish."

The guard opened the gate. He stepped outside. I followed him to the first floor. Without ceremony he pushed the door and we looked in. There was a sudden rustle of movement. We entered and saw that we had disturbed an Igorot family at breakfast. The house was a one-room affair furnished with homemade wooden furniture.

I looked the family over carefully. There was no mistaking those stolid features, dark staring eyes, and wild black hair.

"There is no place for anyone to hide," the assistant superintendent assured me.

He led me outside and down the cobbled walk to the next entrance. The place was a duplicate of the first and the families might have been twins. The same was true of all the quarters in that building.

We walked across the road to the other tenements. I was beginning to feel like a fool. All of the lodgings were the same.

There was no sign of Tampa. When we finished our tour people were beginning to come out their quarters. Two husky Igorot men were entering through the gate.

I saw a girl walking across the inner courtyard with a basket on her head. I was wondering why she would be going to work carrying a basket. I saw her stumble over a loose stone. And then I knew.

Igorot women have an easy grace of carriage. They start carrying baskets on their head when they are three. And they never stumble.

I tore through the gate and ran up to the girl and swung her around, knocking the basket to the ground. In a brief flash I recognize the sunburned face, tousled brown hair and startled blue eyes. The eyes decided me. They were Clem's eyes.

"Tampa!" I said.

And then the riot broke loose.

From the inside of the depot emerged two figures that I knew too well. Bruiser and Killer. Killer ran to the gate and belted it shut. Bruiser turned with his gun and aimed at me. The guards at the gate seemed taken aback by the sudden turn of affairs. They appeared undecided whether to level their guns at us or at each other. The assistant superintendent, locked outside the gate, was shouting orders at nobody in particular.

I made a flying tackle and caught Bruiser around the knees. We rolled over and over. He tried to kick me in the stomach, but I pawed at his arm until I got a good grip on the wrist that held the gun. I twisted the wrist until I heard the gun clatter on the cobblestones. He grunted and kicked me in the shoulder. I landed against a door. I saw him get up to his feet, looking around for the gun. But it was gone. I staggered to my feet and made another running leap at him, butting him in the stomach with my head. He fell on the ground with a heavy thud.

I looked towards the gate, wondering why there had been no gun play. The sight there made me think of figures in a tableau. Inyan was leaning over the gate, his arm wrapped around one guard's neck, pulling tighter and tighter until the fellow lolled helplessly. The gun had dropped to the ground.

The Kalinga hunter was twisting Killer's arms behind his back. With his other hand he pressed a knife at the gunsel's throat.

The other guard had been knocked out. He slumped motionless on the ground. The assistant superintendent was not in sight.

Tampa ran up to me and pushed Bruiser's gun into my hand. We ran towards the gate and slid back the belt. I picked up the guard's gun on my way out. As we ran out of the courtyard, I saw the superintendent lying in a pool of blood.

I pushed Tampa into the jeep and shouted to my friends. "Come on. We've got guns."

Inyan and the hunter leaped from the gate and made for the jeep. I started the motor. There was no place to swing the car around in the narrow road. As we shot backwards down the road. I saw Killer point his gun towards us. Inyan fired. Killer doubled up with a cry and fell flat on his face.

We reached the junction where the road met the mountain highway. We started climbing the sharp incline.

"Did you kill the other one?" Inyan asked.

"Just knocked him out!" I said.

"Then he will be after you," said Inyan.

# TWENTY

Inyan took the wheel. We headed for the airport. During the wild ride over the rough mountain roads, I kept looking back to see if we were being followed. We arrived in Baguio without any sign of pursuit. I settled back in the jeep and sighed with relief. The airport was only a few miles out of Baguio, on the other side of the city.

Inyan and his friend left us at the airport. We said good-bye hastily. I promised them that I would return when our troubles were settled. Then Tampa and I went inside. I found that the one and only flight to Manila was due within an hour.

"Our coffee shop is open," said the clerk. "You could have breakfast while you wait."

Breakfast sounded like a good idea especially after my sitting-up exercises with Bruiser. Tampa and I entered the restaurant and took a table.

It was my first chance to have a good look at her. There could never be any doubt of her Anglo-Saxon ancestry. Her body was at the stage of development where it had lost the gangling angles and was beginning to fill out with soft curves. Her hair was light brown, bleached lighter by years in the tropical sun. Her cheekbones were dotted with freckles and her long straight nose was sunburned. It dawned on me that I had been looking for a youngster and had found a girl on the edge of womanhood, a girl who was strangely breathtaking. It made me realize again how many years had passed since I had gone away.

"It's funny," Tampa was saying, and her diction had a funny little accent. "When you went away I was too young to carry a clear picture of you in my mind. But Dad always spoke about you and this morning, I knew you right away. I felt that you would find me. And now you are here."

I patted her sunbrowned hand. "You've had a rough time, Tampa," I said. "Things will be different when we get to Manila."

She toyed with her food, lost in abstraction. Then she said, "I knew the other man who came to Baung-Baung wasn't you. He was light-complexioned, but I knew he was not an American. I became frightened, and asked the chief to hide me."

"I wonder how Bruiser and Killer found you at the mine," I said.

"Who," she asked.

"Those are my private names for those two toughs. They belong to an outfit that were collaborators during the war.

"The superintendent told me that they had gone there to protect me. They said a big man from Manila wanted to see me, but that someone else would try and kidnap me," Tampa passed her hand over her eyes. "I was so mixed up I didn't know what to believe. I didn't like them, but I was frightened and agreed to hide. Then, when I saw you, I felt I could trust you."

"Poor kid," I said, "no wonder you were afraid of those goons. It was either through them or through Pepe that the assassin was hired to kill your father."

"Who's Pepe?"

"That is the fellow who came to Baung-Baung using my name. He stole the bronze ring from me for that purpose."

Tampa pushed her fork around a fried egg. She stared into space.

"It's funny about him," she said. "I didn't talk to him. I kept out of sight while he was there, but I saw him and heard him. He seemed to be very upset over Dad's death."

Up until now her emotions had seemed buried under a state of shock. Suddenly her eyes filled with tears. I gripped her hand.

"Hold it for a little while, Tampa," I said, "Hold it till we get home to Manila."

I shoved my handkerchief at her and changed the subject.

"I'd give anything to know what was in the letter that Pepe got," I said. "Darn it all, he's come out ahead on this deal in every way."

Tampa blew her nose and looked at me. Then she smiled. "There's one thing he didn't get," she said. "I still have the money belt."

"What money belt?"

"The commando who was to meet Dad during the war had a money belt on him. I found his body and took it off. Dad had been wounded, so I put the belt on myself. I've worn it ever since."

I stared at her, "Didn't you use any of it?"

"Only a very little during the war. But there are several hundred thousands of dollars."

"And you still have it?"

"I wear it under my dress," she said. "Only Dad knew about it."

I threw back my head and started to laugh, not because it was funny, but because I was too tense.

"Now the picture is beginning to make sense," I said. "Now I know why Montalvo and Pepe were trying hard to keep me from seeing Clem. Now I can see why they posted those thugs to get you, too. They wanted to silence Clem because somewhere they had heard about the money, and they wanted it." I grinned at her. "Tampa, finish your breakfast. We still have a job to do. When we get to Manila, we're going to turn that money over to the Army Headquarters. And what a story we will tell them!"

We finished breakfast and went back to the waiting room. There was a long line in front of the ticket counter. I started across the room to take my place in the line. Suddenly I stopped. Ahead of me, five customers away, I saw the short thick neck and broad shoulders of a man who looked familiar. He turned his head slightly, and I know there was no mistake. I recognized his beefy jawline and protruding underlip.

Montalvo.

I groaned.

It meant that we could not take the plane. There was only one flight and I wasn't going to take any risk. Not with Tampa and her money belt.

I got out in a hurry and rejoined Tampa.

"Come on," I told her, "we'll have to take a bus. The wrong people are riding that plane."

Tampa understood at once. She hurried along beside me. We found a taxi. I told the driver to take us to the bus station. Along the way I saw a telegraph office. I had the driver stop. I knew Candy was worried.

I wrote her a message. "Arriving with Tampa tonight," I chewed my pencil a minute. I wanted her to know that we had the money so that she could call Army Headquarters. Finally, I added, "We found a belt. Call Army HQ."

I knew Candy would understand. I paid for the message and went back to the cab.

The plane service in Baguio was skimpy, but there was no shortage of buses.

The bus line is the only service that runs on schedule in the Philippines. The owners are very proud of the fact that the bus leaves promptly ever hour. But when it arrives at a destination is altogether a different matter. The driver goes fast or slow, as he feels inclined, but it is usually fast. If a carabao pulling a squeaky oxcart ties up traffic, nobody complains. And nobody gets impatient. Everybody eats and laughs and talks politics.

Tampa might have impressed me with her sudden maturity, but when it came to eating she was like a growing youngster. During the trip she consumed a big bag of peanuts, a whole bunch of bananas, five pieces of pan dolce, six cokes, several hardboiled eggs and a few candy bars. And at noon she put away a hefty lunch.

"I haven't had any of these things for so long," she apologized. "They taste so good."

"Wait till we get to Manila and then you can wrap your teeth around a real steak," I told her.

I was trying to imagine Tampa dolled up in an evening dress, and she and Candy and I stepping out. Thinking of Candy led me back to Clem.

"I can't understand why Clem didn't write to Candy after the war," I said. "He must have know she was waiting for him. Was he ashamed because he was paralyzed?"

Her face sobered. She munched thoughtfully on some peanuts, hurling the shells out of the window.

"Dad seemed very bitter. He used to say civilization was all rotten and corrupt and that he never wanted to see it again."

"But why did he make you live in the mountains? Why didn't he send you to Candy? And what about your education?"

"I went to school in the village. The son of the chief had been to college. He tutored me. Besides," she added with a smile. "I would never have left Dad."

"I supposed not," I said, patting her hand. "It's hard for me to imagine Clem feeling the way he did. The war must have affected his mind."

"It might have, because he would never talk about it," said Tampa. "Even with me."

It was late afternoon now and the driver was pushing full speed ahead. I knew he would reach Manila before dark, even if he knocked the wind out of all of us. We bounced on the hard bench and clung to each other to steady ourselves. I was a little surprised at the tingle that Tampa's hand gave me. I dropped her hand and hung on the seat, half-ashamed of the sudden warmth that permeated through my body.

It was sunset when we reached Manila. The driver romped through the town, making turns on two wheels, and pulled up at the depot with a flourish. He emitted a loud sigh when he shut off the motor. Everybody sighed happily.

We had beaten nightfall and the terror on the highway after dark. We were back in the city that is as new as air conditioning, as old and wicked as Paris. The city of gaiety and warm laughter and rhumba dancing. And of thugs and footpads and whining beggars. It is a city that whispers over its shoulder at dusk and greets the sunrise with relief. A city of priests and workers, of useless idle women and scheming men, whose mark of affluence is measured by the number of their queridas. It is a city that never sleeps, but which hides itself in the darkness behind barred windows, watching the shadows that stalk in the night.

Taxis were lined up in the compound of the bus depot. Drivers were trying to outscream each other in their efforts to attract the attention of prospective passengers. We took a cab. Soon we were clumping over the cobblestone towards Quezon Boulevard. Tampa leaned forward, looking out of the window. Surprise filled her eyes.

"How desolate it looks!" she said when we passed the ruins of an old stone mansion. "I hadn't imagine it would be this bad."

"It isn't the same city since the war," I told her. "Everything is changed, including the people. It used to be a city of childlike happiness. Now it is full of distrust. Everybody is ready to stick a knife in you."

I was surprised at my own words. It dawned on me that this was the culmination of my experience since I had come back. The bitter lesson which every prodigal learns: that he can never see things again with the eyes of childhood.

We finally reached Candy's house. It was dark now. I paid the driver. Tampa and I ran to the door. I had barely touched the bell when the door opened and Candy smiled at us on the threshold.

She pulled Tampa into her arms, looking at me over Tampa's shoulder.

"Clem?"

"He's dead, Candy." I said.

She took the news without changing the expression in her face. She breathed heavier for a minute, that was all. Then she brightened up and said, "Let's go up to your room and talk."

Tampa had already run ahead into the sala and stood looking around as if she were drinking in the wonder of seeing curtains and cushions and furniture and rugs again. I took Candy's arm and turned towards the sala.

"Later," I said.

"Can't we go now?" she coaxed. "I want to hear all about it from you."

"What's the matter?" I laughed. "I've brought you a daughter and you want to leave her already?" I lowered my voice. "We must be good to Tampa. She's been through a lot."

Candy looked at me with a strange expression in her eyes. Then she's swallowed hard and followed me unwillingly into the sala. She poured me a drink and interrupted me.

"You really have the money belt, Tampa?" she asked.

"Yes," said Tampa.

"How much?"

"Several hundred thousand dollars."

"American dollars?" asked Candy.

"Of course," laughed Tampa. "It was to be distributed during the war among the guerillas."

"Did you call the Army Headquarters?" I asked.

I was sitting with my back to the kitchen. As if my words were a signal, I heard the door behind me open. Then a voice said, "You don't have to worry about the money any longer. I'll take charge of it."

I swung to my feet. The drink was still in my hand. I saw Montalvo with a gun pointed at me. I looked over his shoulder to see if Bruiser and Killer were behind. He smiled grimly.

"You needn't worry about my assistants. This is a private party. Give me the money belt."

I threw the glass in his face and jumped for the gun. There was a loud report. A streak of hot flame shook my right shoulder. I fell on the floor.

Then, with my left hand, I grabbed Montalvo's legs.

Suddenly a woman's cold voice said, "It's no use, Gar. I have you covered."

I let go of Montalvo and turned around.

Candy was pointing a gun at me.

# TWENTY-ONE

I stared at Candy. The thought flashed across my mind that I had not heard her right. But I could not deny that she stood before me now pointing a snub-nosed gun. Her face was transformed into bitter lines. I got up from the floor, holding the spreading red on my shoulder. I was becoming dizzy.

Montalvo moved. The highball was still dripping on his face. His urbanity had deserted him. He had become brisk and businesslike.

"Take the girl into the other room," he ordered Candy, "and get that belt."

Candy took Tampa's arm and pushed her into the kitchen. There was a little tussle. Then I heard a slap. When they returned on Tampa's cheek was a bright scratch. Candy had the belt. She opened it and looked inside and a smile lighted up her face.

"Hurry up," said Montalvo.

"Candy, don't do it," I pleaded. "Is this what Clem died for?"

She looked at me bitterly.

"I didn't want it done this way," she said. "I had planned that you and I would enjoy it together."

"You planned this?" I said.

Montalvo laughed. "Of course she did. That's what she used you for. She had to find her husband to silence him. Otherwise she would have been brought to trial with the others."

I stared at Candy incredulously. "You collaborated during the war?"

Candy looked from Tampa to me like an animal at bay. Then she said, "Yes, I did. It was the only way I could get money for clothes and decent food. It's all very well to be noble and wave a flag, but I couldn't live in a pigsty."

I still couldn't get it through my head.

"You've been working with Montalvo all this time?" I demanded.

Candy hesitated, but Montalvo answered for her.

"Of course, Candy stirred up more than she realized when she started searching for her husband. When word of your activities reached up my ears, I had to intervene in order to protect all of us. It wasn't until after you escaped from my men on the sugarcane plantation that she told me about the money. She made a deal with me to spare your life until you secured it for us." He looked at me with cool amusement. "I'll say this for you Americans. You are so thick-skinned you can take any punishment when you start after something. By the way, how did you escape from that plantation?"

I didn't answer. I was staring at Candy, my illusions of twenty years shattered.

"So you were the one behind all this," I said.

"You're a fool, Gar," said Candy. "You could have had all this and me, too."

I stared at her in bitter silence.

"I asked you a question," began Montalvo harshly.

Candy interrupted him. "Oh, stop playing dictator," she said. "We got what we were after." She ran her fingers over the money belt. "Now, I can leave this country and have all the nice things I want."

Montalvo reached out for the belt.

"You mean we are leaving the country, my dear," he said. "And we will enjoy this together." He took the belt and rolled it up and stuffed it in his pocket. "As long as I keep this," he told her, "I know I will always have you." He aimed his gun at me. "Let's get this over with and be on our way."

Candy stepped in front of him.

"Don't do it," she said. "You promised."

"You are too tenderhearted, my dear," said Montalvo. "You can have your husband murdered, but you can't shoot your friend."

Then Montalvo swung around and hit me on the head with the butt of his gun. I fell down again. Darkness was slowly surrounding me.

"Hurry," said Montalvo. "The launch is waiting."

I heard Candy run into the kitchen. She came back with stout cord and towels. Tampa sat passively when Candy bound and gagged her. Then Candy turned to me.

I could not say anything. In fact all the fight had gone out of me. I had the feeling that this was all a nightmare and that presently I would wake up and tell Candy all about it and we would laugh together. But the enfolding darkness was making me sway.

At the door Candy turned to look at me, and said again, "I didn't want it done this way."

Montalvo grasped her arm and pulled her outside.

I shook the darkness away and rolled to the floor. I floundered around and finally made it to my knees. The darkness in my mind was gradually drifting away. I crawled to the window. I pulled at the blind with my teeth. Then I saw them.

They crossed the street to Montalvo's car. I wondered if Damyan was driving. I pushed away the last shreds of darkness from my mind, wondering why they did not drive away. A narrow beam of light revealed Montalvo and another figure bending over the right front wheel. Yes, the other man was Damyan.

Montalvo looked up towards the window, spraying glass over me. I looked at Tampa, but she was unhurt. Slowly, I got up on my knees and bit the curtain. Then I heard the car roll away. The curtain snapped off the roller. I fell down backwards.

I was still rolling on the floor and trying to get up on my knees when I heard a car stop in front of the house. I rolled to the window and got up by sliding my back against the wall. Several cars pulled up and policemen were piling out. Two figures ran towards the front door. I could not see their faces, but one of them stopped long enough to point his finger at me and laugh. The voice sounded familiar. The man who laughed beckoned to the men. Four of them came to the door and tried to break it down.

I rolled towards the door. Then I heard someone say, "We'll have to shoot the lock."

There was a loud report. The door burst open and they came in with drawn guns. Then I saw someone that gave me another shock.

Pepe was walking beside a Filipino colonel. He started to laugh again when he saw me. Goyo was trailing behind. One of the police cut my bonds.

"Hurt bad?" Pepe asked.

"Just my shoulder." I said.

They freed Tampa, and one of the men, who looked like a doctor, ripped off my coat and daubed some fluid in the wound. The medicine stung and made me dizzy for a minute.

"You are lucky," he said, patting a wad of cotton and adhesive tape on the wound. And he laughed. "Half an hour longer and you would have bled to death."

I laughed too. The loss of blood made my head light. Suddenly it seemed very funny to me that I had just escaped bleeding to death. Somebody pushed some brandy down my throat. I stopped laughing.

"It looks like we're late," said Pepe. "Do you know which way they were going?"

"Montalvo spoke of a launch waiting," I said.

"We'll try the pier," said Pepe. He turned to the colonel and gave some order. The colonel saluted and said. "Yes, sir."

The plot was getting thicker. Nobody seemed to fit into the roles I had assigned them. Candy had turned out to be a conspirator and Pepe was giving orders to a colonel. I ran my fingers through my hair.

"Everything is upside down," I said to Pepe.

Pepe laughed again.

Goyo smiled and said. "He belongs to the Philippine Intelligence."

"I haven't time to tell you everything now," said Pepe. "Are you strong enough to come with us? You're in this pretty deep and you deserve a chance to see the finale."

"You bet I want to see it," I said. I turned to Tampa. "Come on, Tampa. You don't want to stay here alone.

We hurried outside and piled into a car. Pepe posted two policemen at the house. When we came up to Dewey Boulevard the driver turned on the siren and the car rolled at a breakneck speed.

We swung left, past the Manila Hotel towards the ruins of the old Walled City.

There we saw ahead of us the red taillight of a car standing in the middle of the road. Our headlights picked up the figure of Damyan bent over the motor. He straightened up. He grinned and pointed towards the pier. We swung toward the pier and saw Montalvo and Candy running with their suitcases. They dropped their suitcases and fled towards the edge of the dock. Our searchlight glared on them. They started climbing down the wooden ladder to the launch waiting below.

The policeman in the front seat raised his gun. Pepe leaned forward and touched his arm.

"Careful with your aim," he said. "We want them alive."

The policeman fired. He missed. Candy and Montalvo were stepping into the launch when we pulled up. Montalvo raised his gun and fired. He got the policeman.

Pepe jumped out of the car and fired back. Then several guns barked. Montalvo yelled and fell on his face. Candy tried to start the motor. Pepe's gun barked again. Candy screamed and stood up, firing blindly. She lost her balance and fell overboard.

Several policeman jumped into the launch. Two of the men dived into the water after her. Another ran down the ladder to help Pepe pick up Montalvo. He was still alive. They laid Candy on the deck. She was dead.

I turned away. I didn't care about the rest of the drama. I found a cigarette and lit it and stood smoking it blindly. Someone touched my arm.

It was Pepe. He was not smiling now.

"It's all over," he said quietly. "Shall we go back to the house?"

I nodded. I followed him silently to the car. We climbed in and sat beside Tampa.

"I don't believe I know this young lady," said Pepe.

"I forgot the amenities," I said. "This is Tampa Mayo. Clem's daughter."

Pepe's eyes widened. He gave a low whistle.

"I'm sorry about your father," he told her. "I had hoped to save him, but when I reached Baung-Baung, he was already dead."

"How did you get to Baung-Baung?" I asked.

"When I left you and Inyan asleep in the hut, I went back to the American gas station. I woke up Mr. Mountain and told him that I had to get to Baung-Baung in a hurry, so he sent one of his sons to guide me. Mr. Mountain's wife had originally come from a nearby village."

We reached Candy's house. Only it was Tampa's house now. I stood on the walk for a minute looking at the broken window and busted door. I did not want to go inside. I knew I would find Candy in the house. I knew her perfume would be in the air. I knew the imprint of her body would still be on the cushions. She would be everywhere.

Again it was Pepe who broke my mood. He put his arm around my shoulder and another around Tampa. He led us into the house. Goyo trailed behind.

"How about fixing us a drink, Goyo?" said Pepe.

"Now you're talking," said Goyo. "I'm even better as a bartender than as a pickpocket."

His remark broke the tension. We all laughed.

Then when Goyo handed me a glass, I remembered that I was about to do this very thing earlier in the evening before Candy unveiled her treachery. I shuddered with bitterness and poured the drink down my throat.

There was a soft knock on the door. Damyan came in with the colonel. He walked to Pepe and gave him the money belt. Pepe looked at the belt in silence and handed it to the colonel.

Then Pepe said to me. "We almost forgot what all the shooting was about."

I looked up at Pepe and said, "There are still some details I would like to know."

# TWENTY-TWO

Pepe sipped his drink.

"I will begin from the beginning," Pepe said. "I had been assigned by the government to get evidence against the collaborators. The work was not easy. Many of them were among my own friends." His mouth twisted with bitterness. "But the Montalvo gang blocked my way because of their social position and connections in government. But I finally got the evidence I needed. We made another raid earlier this evening and arrested two other men whom you know. Estacio and Ramirez." He sighed. "Now, with the arrest of Montalvo, my job is complete."

I looked at Damyan. Pepe followed my glance.

"Damyan was working with me. He was the head of the Igorot underground and it was through him that my attention was turned to Candy. But it was hard to get evidence against her. There were only rumors to go on, rumors from Igorots who had heard about her collaboration with the enemy during the war. And then Damyan showed me the bronze ring that her husband had sent to him. During the war that ring had been used as a message of great importance on our side. There is only one place where it could come from and its appearance always meant that the guerillas in Baguio wanted help.

"Damyan did not know where the ring came from, but we both felt it was from someone who had evidence against Candy. So we placed the ring on display in the store where she shopped regularly. And the ring did the trick. She became panicky. She realized that her husband was still alive. She was afraid that her treachery would come to light, that she had betrayed Clem and the commando." Pepe paused and lit a cigarette. "I did not count on her sending for you, and I was upset when I first saw you. I didn't know what side you were on, so for a while I just watched you.

"And Montalvo was alert, too. At first he thought he could buy you off, just as he had bought everything and everybody. Then he decided you were with intelligence. And I'm afraid I encouraged him in the idea." Pepe grinned.

"I am sorry you had to be roughed up, but I know that if Montalvo concentrated on you, I would be given a free hand."

"And all the time," I said, "I thought you were tied up with Montalvo. I guess it was because you all belong to the same country club."

"Not all the people with bank accounts are traitors," said Pepe. "And if this country is ever going to get on its feet, some of us have to take an honest stand."

"Tell me one thing," I said. "What was on that paper Rosa Linkhow gave you?"

Pepe threw back his head and laughed.

"Oh, boy! You really scared the wits out of Rosa that night," he laughed. "You see, Rosa was losing out with Montalvo. He had transferred his affections to Candy. And Rosa, to get even with him, gave me evidence of his transactions with the Japs during the war. Any more questions?"

"What was in Clem's letter that was intended for me?" I asked.

"I'm sorry I had to open your mail," said Pepe. "The letter contained the whole story of Candy's treachery. You see, everything she did in Baguio was known by the Igorots. Her own cook was watching her. After the commando and Clem were betrayed, the Igorots told Clem about it. That was why after the war he would not return to her. He knew her greed for money and that someday she would start hunting for the money belt."

"Do you think she had Clem murdered?" I asked.

"In the beginning," Pepe said, "all she wanted was the money. Then Montalvo heard about it. He forced her to play along with him. Oh, Candy was a great actress. My guess is that up to the very last she intended to doublecross Montalvo and take the money and ship out with you, if she could persuade you."

"Now, I understand," I said, "why she was trying to hurry me up to Baguio. She wanted me to get the money before Montalvo heard about it. Even tonight when we walked in she tried to keep me out of the sala. When she saw it was no use, she threw her lot in with him." We were silent for a moment. "By the way, after Clem's death, why didn't you go after the money?" I asked.

"There wasn't time. When I got the evidence, I knew I had to hurry to Manila to press charges. I knew you would look for Tampa until you found her. Anyway, you gave yourself away when you sent Candy that wire about the belt. One of my men was planted in the telegraph office. When I got the news, I knew there was no time to be lost. I knew that once they had the money they would try to leave the country."

"Is Goyo working with you also?" I asked.

Goyo right now was having the time of his life with the liquor supply. He had the table littered with bottles and was sampling Cointreau, brandy, Crème de Menthe and scotch.

"No," said Pepe. "Goyo is another one who gave me some bad moments. Because he got around everywhere, he heard a good many things. He found Damyan before I was ready for you to meet Damyan. In fact, that day at the Quiapo Market you would have met Damyan if I had not stopped you."

"You were always showing up in the wrong places," I said.

"Sometimes I showed up too late," said Pepe soberly. "Like the night the nightclub singer was killed. I was almost too late tonight, too. I got tied up in Baguio over the case of that hunter who killed Mayo, and I had to get a private plane to take me back." He stood up and laid his hand on my shoulder and smiled down at me. "You two have to help each other." He raised his glasses and toasted us, "Salud, fortuna y amor."

"What's that again?" I asked.

Pepe laughed. "You should never forget the famous toast of Manila. It's the toast that offers everything. Salud, fortuna y amor. Health, wealth and love!"

He turned to Tampa. "I will take you to my sister's tonight," he said. "Goyo will stay with Gar."

She nodded and got up. I walked with them to the door and pressed her hand.

"Get some rest," I told her. "Tomorrow you must go shopping."

Her eyes lighted up. I watched them leave the house, then I turned and looked at Candy's living room again. Then I noticed Goyo still busy sampling drinks. I decided he had the right idea. I pulled up a chair and sat down beside him and looked at the line of bottles.

"Which way are you working, to the left or right?" I asked.

He stopped drinking long enough to point in the general direction of right.

"Okay," I said. "I'll work from right to left and meet you in the middle."

I was wrong. We didn't meet in the middle. We met under the table next morning.

The Montalvo gang trial is now over and I am happy that the old man was found guilty and sentenced to be executed. Estacio and Ramirez got off a little lighter with twenty years apiece.

Damyan has changed jobs. He is working now for Pepe. He received so much publicity during Montalvo's trial that everybody in town was afraid to hire him.

The most amusing development is Goyo. He has taken up an honest trade. I taught him to drive, and employed him as my chauffeur. The only trouble is he hasn't yet learned that there is a speed slower than sixty miles an hour. But he makes a good drinking companion on long evenings, so when we get in the car I just close my eyes and hope for the best.

Tampa is in the United States now. She receive a big-sized reward from Uncle Sam for turning in the money belt. So she went to Berkeley to study at the University of California.

I am still here in Manila. I am trying to dispose of my property. Maybe someday I will return Stateside. Maybe I will go back to the docks of San Francisco, the Embarcadero, the cable cars, the paved streets, the strikes and the ten-cent stores.

I don't know.

It all depends on what Tampa says in answer to my last letter. I told her that she was seventeen and getting along in years and that two could go to college as cheaply as one, and did she want to be an old maid all her life? I also told her if she liked the idea of listening to my harmonica music to reply by air mail.

As I write this somebody is ringing the doorbell. Lening comes in and hands me a cable. It's from Berkeley.

Now, that's a woman for you. Airmail means "yes," regular mail means "no." What the hell is a cable?

I am sitting here and turning it over in my hands. I'm afraid to open it.

# THE FILIPINO HOUSEBOY

When Dunstan Peyton was rummaging in his favorite bookshop, he found a book written by his former Filipino houseboy. He was somewhat amused because when the houseboy left him fifteen years before, he had said something about going into the writing business. Peyton had not given it a thought at the time. But as he opened the book, he was thrilled with envy. He discovered that the houseboy had written several books, and two of them had been reviewed favorably by critics and made considerable sales. He bought them all and went home, remembering back to the years when Conrado Bustamante was in his employ.

Dunstan Peyton had written a novel which was bought by one of the Hollywood movie studios for what he then considered a great sum of money. And that was how he went to Hollywood, lucky to have a five-year contract, lucky to escape from his small dark room in Brooklyn. As soon as he had settled himself in a house, he was advised by his new friends to have a Filipino houseboy. These friends had Filipino houseboys themselves, so they were in the position to appraise the qualities and virtues of houseboys. He understood from them that Filipino houseboys were neat, efficient, courteous and inexpensive. Well, he consented.

Conrado went to Dunstan Peyton's house through the amazing chain of circumstances that is common among houseboys in Hollywood and Beverly Hills. One of Dunstan's friends told his Filipino houseboy about his need, so the houseboy passed it on to his friends; and the next morning, before Dunstan had had his coffee, Conrado appeared at the door.

Dunstan had expected an older man. He was confronted by a Filipino who was probably nineteen. And of course he was small and frail, but he had a pleasant smile through which peeped out well-formed clean teeth. His suit was immaculate gray, new, well-tailored and expensive. And his hat, which he had alertly taken off his black head when Dunstan opened the door, was dove-colored, new, wide-brimmed, and expensive. He also had an expensive briefcase in his left hand, and Dunstan wondered if he really needed a job. He was barely five feet tall, and perhaps weighed less than a hundred pounds on bare feet. He had small twinkling eyes that slanted merrily upward when he smiled. Dunstan was sold right away.

"Mr. Dunstan Peyton?" he asked.

"Yes."

"I am the houseboy, sir," he announced himself.

"Come in."

He walked into the living room and put the briefcase on the nearest table. Then he introduced himself, "My name is Conrado Bustamante. Call me Conrad, Sir."

Dunstan liked the easy frankness of the little fellow. Although he had heard that he should not be too intimate with servants, he offered his hand. Conrad took it warmly. Then he opened his briefcase, and out came kitchen tools, sharp carving knives, roasting forks, a blue apron, and a tall white hat. He took off his coat and hung it on the chair, put his dove-colored hat beside the briefcase, and immediately wrapped the apron around him. The tall white hat leaped to his head, and for a moment he stood at attention for Dunstan's inspection, faintly smiling; then he was on his way to the kitchen with his cooking paraphernalia. In another minute he was preparing breakfast, moving about the place as though he were intimate with it. He knew exactly what drawer to open when he needed something.

Dunstan stood at the kitchen door and watched him with amazement. And he wondered if his friend had given him an expensive houseboy. It was his first time to have a servant, so he wanted to discuss the question of wages immediately.

"Conrad," he said.

"Yes, Mr. Peyton?"

"About your salary, Conrad. We have not discussed it."

"It is not important, Mr. Peyton," he answered. "We will discuss it later."

"I have many things on my mind, Conrad. I would like to settle this problem and forget about it. How much would you like?"

"I leave it to you, Mr. Peyton."

Dunstan felt cheap. But he let it go at that, and went upstairs to put on his clothes. He was due at the studio at eleven, and it was already nine. When he went down to the breakfast room, he saw the neatly prepared table. Conrad had placed a vase of assorted flowers on the table, and suddenly Dunstan realized that Conrad had gone out to the backyard and cut all sorts of flowering plants that former tenants had planted there, near the palm trees and bananas. He sat down and sighed.

Conrad came out of the kitchen with the coffee. Without the apron and the tall white hat, of course, for he had on a white jacket and a black tie. It was a perfect setup, and the breakfast was really good, and the whole atmosphere was bright and cheery and clean. Dunstan looked forward to a life of comfort and pleasure.

When he finished breakfast, he rushed to the door. And Conrad was there, too, opening the door with a smile and wishing him well. For a moment he was tempted to discuss Conrad's salary again, but the well-meaning brown face halted him. And again he felt cheap. He went to his car and drove away, trying to forget his engaging houseboy.

It was Dunstan's first conference with studio executives, and he was new in the game. But they finally came to an agreement, to the satisfaction of everybody. It was already ten in the evening when he drove into the yard of his house. There was a car in the driveway and a Filipino, who was definitely not Conrad, was carrying boxes and suitcases from it and taking them into the house. He was taller than Conrad and bigger of body and perhaps a few years older. He parked the car in the driveway and went into the house.

Conrad met him in the living room and took his hat and coat. "Good evening, sir," he greeted him.

"Good evening, Conrad," Dunstan said. Then he said, "There is a car in the driveway."

"Oh yes, Mr. Peyton," he answered. "It is my cousin Danny's car. He is bringing my things. I will tell him to make way for you, sir."

"Never mind," he said. "Here is the key to the car. When he is ready to pull out, put the car in the garage."

"Yes, sir."

"I'm going upstairs for a minute. Let me know when the dinner is ready."

"It is ready, Mr. Peyton."

"Well, keep it burning."

"It is burning, sir. I will show you."

The small guy was irresistible. Dunstan followed him into

the dining room. And, lo and behold, his dinner was really burning on the table. Conrad had acquired from somewhere one of those Japanese stoves on which they cook sukiyaki. It is the Japanese custom to cook sukiyaki on the dining table, so that the divers should have the pleasure of preparing the dish themselves or watch the cook do it; and in that way the food is really fresh and warm and appetizing. Dunstan looked at the strange setup and almost laughed. And his steak, smothered with onions and mushrooms, looked so delicious that he was tempted to eat without cleaning himself. He told Conrad to keep it burning and went upstairs.

When he return to the dining room everything was ready. The onions and mushrooms had been chopped and mixed in the gravy. The steak was sizzling hot. And of course Conrad was gone, and his cousin had taken his place. He was wearing a white jacket and a black tie.

"Good evening, sir," he greeted Dunstan's. "My name is Daniel Manansala. Danny for short, sir."

"Good evening, Danny," he said, sitting down. "Where is Conrad?"

"He is in the kitchen, sir." And when he noticed Dunstan's consternation, he added, "I am just helping him, sir."

"That is nice of you, Danny. Thank you."

"Would you like to have dinner now?"

"Yes,"

Danny unhooked the stove and put the steak in Dunstan's plate. Then he went to the kitchen and came back with a clay pitcher. He poured the water from the pitcher into the drinking glass and started to serve Dunstan. Dunstan had not noticed the clay pitcher before, but he took it for granted that it was one of Conrad's acquisitions from the Japanese, like the sukiyaki stove. The steak was good. The fried potatoes were good, too. As Dunstan ate he tried to get acquainted with Danny. He noticed that Conrad and Danny spoke English fluently, although with a slight accent that seemed to him of Spanish tinge.

"Are you employed somewhere, Danny?" Dunstan asked.

"No, sir. Jobs are very scarce."

"Some people are lucky, like myself."

"I know, sir."

"What kind of work do you do?"

"Well, I do all kinds of things. But I am really a bartender by profession."

"I hope you will find a job soon, Danny."

"Thank you, sir."

He wanted to ask him about his education, but that would be too much prying into his private life. He had often thought that Filipino spoke pidgin English, like in the movies, but here were two of them who used the language more eloquently than some Americans. He concluded silently that Danny and Conrad had gone to American colleges. (Later he discovered that he was wrong. Conrad had one year of high school in the Philippines, while Danny had gone only to the sixth grade.) They did not act the way servants are supposed to act; they were respectful, but not subservient. He did not want to act like a master, either. So he enjoyed the arrangement, but he tried to hide his satisfaction.

After dinner Dunstan went to the library to read the book he was assigned to make a report on. Conrad took over. He came in with a tray, and it was a bowl of ice and one half of a pineapple, and in the pineapple were slices of banana, pineapple meat, apple and pear, and underneath this combination was a generous supply of rum. Dunstan ate the fruit and sipped the drink. It was good, and it was strong, and it warmed him from head to toe.

"That was a good dinner, Conrad," he said.

"I am glad you like it, sir."

"The stove is a bright idea. It is Japanese, is it not?"

"Yes, sir."

"Where did you get it?"

"I got it from a Japanese friend. I used to live with a Japanese family, Mr. Peyton."

"You did? Where?"

"In Goleta, sir. A small town north of Santa Barbara. About seven miles north, by the sea."

"What were you doing with a Japanese family?"

"I worked with them in the field. The old man was a farmer. But they all worked, including the children, after school hours of course."

"How are they? I mean the Japanese people."

"They are like other people. They have a strange ways, like bathing in the nude in the family tub, a large wooden tub with the fire going on underneath."

"You mean all of them"

"Yes, sir. Men, women, and children. All nude."

"They could get arrested for that."

"I guess so, sir. But that is their way to economize water and firewood."

"Did you bathe with them?"

"Oh yes. I used to be ashamed, but they took that away from me. The girls would grab me and undress me and throw me into the tub. I used to hide my private [parts] with my hand, but they took that away from me too. Later, however, I realized that they had the right idea."

"I should say so." Dunstan finished the drink, and it was really good. "I like the drink, Conrad. Will you make another?"

"Yes, sir. It is my cousin's concoction. He is a bartender."

"That is what he told me."

"I will tell him to make another, sir."

When Conrad came back Dunstan told him goodnight and went upstairs with the drink. It was an hour later when he heard the guitar from Conrad's room. Then there was a violin. He listened to the duet. It was a song unknown to him, a very sad song, and it seemed far away. He was curious which one was playing what instrument. He went downstairs and knocked on Conrad's door.

Conrad opened it. Danny was on the bed; he had the guitar. Conrad had the violin.

"Are we bothering you, Mr. Peyton?" Conrad asked Dunstan.

"No, Conrad," he said. "I was just curious which one was playing what instrument. Now I know. You are both very good."

"Will you sit down, sir?" Danny said.

Dunstan sat down on the only chair in the room. "What were you playing?" he asked Conrad.

"It is a Philippine song, Mr. Peyton," Conrad answered. "It is called kundiman, or love song. A very sad song, Filipinos are very sad people."

"I didn't know that, Conrad, Why?"

"They have never been free, that is why, Mr. Peyton."

The Dunstan noticed that Conrad's voice had indeed become sad. His whole face changed, his eyes became luminous. And the sudden remembrance of their people had affected Danny, too. And Dunstan knew that he had to break the silence.

"Will you go on with the song?" he told them. "I like to hear it."

"Okay, Danny?" Conrad said to his cousin.

Danny nodded his head. Conrad stood in front of Danny, who was still sitting on the bed, and the sad music began. As Dunstan watched them he realized that music was what Filipinos had to comfort themselves, since they had nothing else, and it was a good thing. They had no women of their own, and they had no families. They had no homes and they had no country. They were exiles. Their places of birth were far away, and they brought with them some memories of their land, and these were in their music. It was the only tangible thread that they had with their people, and it was a marvelous bridge to yesterday and their native land. He felt like he was intruding in their secret world, so he got up quietly and went upstairs to his bedroom. It was well toward dawn when they stopped playing.

The next morning Danny served him at breakfast. And it was then that he realized that he had slept in his house. It was something new to Dunstan, and he was apprehensive. Was he serving him to pay for his night's lodging? He could not ask him. But he was delighted. He had two houseboys, and he was paying only for one. He left the house with a wonderful feeling.

Dunstan went home early. And there in the backyard, stripped to the waist, was Danny. He had pulled out the tall weeds and dug the ground. These people were full of surprises.

"Good afternoon, Mr. Peyton," Danny greeted him.

"Good afternoon, Danny," he said. "What are you trying to do with the yard?"

"I will make a garden, sir."

"That is a good idea," I said. "We need a pleasant atmosphere. Flowers and stuff like that, eh?"

"Oh no, sir. I will plant edible things."

144

"I see. Tomatoes and potatoes."

"Oriental stuff, Mr. Peyton. Bitter melons, gourds, eggplants, red peppers and, Chinese greens and string beans. The beans grow as long as four feet."

"Go to it, Danny."

"Yes, sir."

Dunstan went into the house and asked Conrad to fix him a drink. And Danny served him again that evening. Perhaps he will leave tomorrow, Dunstan thought to himself. But he was wrong again. Danny stayed on, taking care of his garden and serving him when Conrad was busy in the kitchen. Dunstan did not bother to ask him when he was leaving. He was getting used to his presence in the house, and he was not paying him anyway.

But he began to worry about the grocery bill. So one Sunday, when they were both in the yard watering their garden, he went to Conrad's room and found two sacks of rice, canned bamboo shoots, fresh bitter melons, strange-looking greens, and dried fish. Then he realized that they had been buying their own groceries and cooking in their own fashion. He was relieved. He had been worrying for nothing.

Strange people, these Filipinos. Then, again, Dunstan was curious how they prepared their own food. And his curiosity was gratified one evening. He was working late on a movie script and he felt tired and sleepy. He went downstairs to ask Danny to make him a drink. And there they were, eating at the kitchen table in their own fashion. With their fingers, of course.

The food look delicious. There was a big bowl of rice, a plate of pork cooked with spices and vinegar, and it was generously browned with paprika. There was also a plate of what looked like thin slices of raw fish.

"Will you fix me a drink, Danny?" he said.

"Yes, sir."

"Are you eating Filipino dishes, Conrad?"

"Filipino and Japanese, Mr. Peyton. The pork is a Filipino dish. We call it adobo. It is a national dish in the Philippines. It is the Filipinization of the Spanish lechon. The fish is a Japanese dish, and it is raw, it is tuna, and the Japanese call the dish sasame. The rice is of course a common dish in the Orient."

Dunstan tasted the pork, and it was really delicious. Bay leaves had given it an enchanting smell. It was a little too hot for him, but he liked it.

"Try the sasame, Mr. Peyton," Conrad suggested. "You will not like it at first, but you will get used to it."

"Maybe it will make me sick, Conrad," I said.

I don't think so, Mr. Peyton. Try a little piece."

Dunstan tasted it, and to his surprise he found it good. It did not taste like fish at all. It was cold and soft, almost like a piece of silk, so he took a bigger piece. He liked it.

"It is good when you are drinking, Mr. Peyton," Conrad said.

"Is that so?"

Yes, sir."

Danny came back with Dunstan's drink just then, and he drank it and ate some more sasame.

"The sasame is good when you are drinking, all right," he said. "But you are not drinking."

"We are drinking, Mr. Peyton," Conrad said, smiling. And bending down, he produced a gallon of port wine. They had covered it with a newspaper under the table. And the glasses were on the table, covered with a dish towel. Very smart and discreet people, Dunstan thought to himself.

Then they were all drinking and eating the sasame. And after a while he got himself a plate and filled it with rice and the adobo. He tried to eat in their fashion, with his fingers of course, but the rice fell on the floor. He abandoned the idea and got himself a fork and knife. Danny fixed him another drink, and Conrad sliced some more tuna. Dunstan wondered what his associates at the studio would think if they saw him eating raw fish with his houseboy and his cousin.

"We also eat raw squid, Mr. Peyton," Conrad said.

"Raw squid? It must be awful."

"When it is prepared right it is good, sir," Danny explained. "But raw chicken meat is better."

"Raw chicken meat?"

"Yes, sir," Conrad said. "We got it from the Japanese. Raw squid is a Filipino idea. At least the Filipinos in this country. There are no squids in the Philippines."

"We also eat raw goat meat," Danny said.

Dunstan's appetite for the sasame was gone. He bade them goodnight and went upstairs, expecting his stomach to be upset. But to his surprise nothing happened. He prepared for bed. He was about to fall asleep when the music began in Conrad's room. Well, he had a free orchestra in his house. He listened and smiled with contentment.

And Danny stayed on. His garden was now a sight to see. The bitter melons were flowering. The eggplants were already the size of a little boy's fist. The gourds were hanging on the sticks. The peppers were yellowing in the sun. And suddenly Dunstan realized that Conrad and Danny had been with him for nearly a month.

One evening he found Conrad giving Danny a haircut in his room. Conrad's hair was already cut: they had given each other a haircut. Dunstan did not realize that Filipinos were also good barbers. They planted their own vegetables, and they cut their own hair. It was good economics. And as he looked at their splendid black heads, he knew that he would ask Conrad to cut his hair.

So the next day Dunstan asked him, and he gave him a haircut. And every week afterward he gave him a haircut, sometimes in the kitchen and at other times in the yard. Dunstan's haircut was so good that one of his associates at the studio asked him about his barber, but when he told him it was his houseboy, he nearly died laughing. Then he suggested that he would try him, and he told Conrad about it, and agreed. Thereafter Conrad had a job in his hands.

Dunstan went home early one day and Conrad announced that his cousin had gone to San Francisco where a job was waiting for him. He felt sorry for Conrad, because now he would be alone. But he was not lonely: he went on playing his violin. Sometimes he played the guitar. He played every night, far into the night.

Dunstan gave his check that week, adding something for his cousin. He looked at the check and frowned. Dunstan thought he had not given him enough, after all the information that he got from his friends who had Filipino houseboys.

"What is the matter, Conrad?" Dunstan asked.

"You gave me too much, Mr. Peyton," he said.

He nearly jumped out of his skin. But he was relieved, too. And it came to him that he would get along with Conrad, and Conrad could stay with him as long as he liked. Conrad's honesty was bewildering, and Dunstan was ashamed for sometimes doubting him.

"Well, Conrad," he said, "I added a little something for your cousin."

"He does not need it, Mr. Peyton. In fact he has just sent me some money for you.'

"For me? Why?"

"For the days that he had stayed at your house, sir."

"That is nice of him, Conrad." Dunstan was really touched by their sincerity. "But you can keep it. And thank him for me, please."

"I will do that, Mr. Peyton."

"And you can keep that check too, as it is."

"Thank you, sir."

Dunstan went upstairs and looked out the window. Danny's garden was now in full bloom. He could not look at the garden again without thinking kindly of Danny. And Conrad, too. Yes, Conrad, who brought humor to his house.

# APPENDIXES

My mind is at its apogee today because I did not have a bout with old
Bacchus this weekend. And the first person I thought of this morning
upon seeing the world thinly covered with white soft things from heaven was you and only you with the small white face. And yesterday morning too, when the first snow of the year came to bless me with its pu-
rity and womanlike softness, when I looked westward from your awakening
city that was not unkind, but in truth enchanting with its whitening faraway horizons.

Now after doing some work today toward the realization of a grand dream which
was once stifled by my own foolhardy way, I thought of you again in connection with my work. It is always heartwarming to awaken with your bright
image in the mirror of my mind, like a new moon stepping down to the threshold of my abode with all her fragrance.

But we don't seem to have enough time any more to hold the face of life
long in our hands, to know it that it is also longing to let its blood
in the veins of our longing. Our days are taken up by so many things
which are sometimes destructive to our longing. As a matter of fact,
when I read your last note last night, I felt that somehow you have not
discovered the exact image and shape of your personality, no matter what
you are doing to reach that penultimate of peace, no matter what inward
excuse you make, because in the end the fragments of yourself will re-
arrange themselves without your knowing.

Why do I write like this? Because I have in a way reached a certain kind
of peace, after so long and after so much sacrifice, when I was young. I
am still sacrificing, but not without my knowledge, which is fair enough
in a world so confused, so troubled, so uncertain. In this connection,
because it is humming in my mind this very moment, you should read Ar-
nold's "Dover Beach", in which he expressed the sentiments of
the Victorian era in such a deeply melancholy tone of verse, that it
it even applies to all mankind, when he was thinking only of England.

And this weekend - if you want to know - I made a list of great novels
that I want to read until I have no more eyes to see. I started it
with one book each from the following: Dreiser, Frank Norris, Stepehn
Crane, London, Samuel Butler. How much we have missed - we who read
only what we call progressive literature. We owe so much from the old
masters, their wide comprehension of human life, the depth of their feel-
ings, their pity and compassion for man, their pride and honor as men
of integrity. Often we dismiss Dreiser and give so much unnecessary
importance to little books such as A LANTERN FOR JEREMY. Dreiser's scope
in the barbaric field of financial maurading, political chicanery and
social snobbery is a dimension which is still unsurpassed, and almost
as broad and deep as Balzac's dissection of French society in his time.
On the other hand, the bourgeoisie, marooned without hope of salvation
in the darkness of their libido, exasperate us with their coddling of
neurotic culture including their cabalistic poetry. When a social system is losing a foothold in the march of progress and civilization, it
also loses its sense of values including the meanings of words, because
they are all irremediably dying. Thus are born many isms in literature,
the death throes of a living dying: so doomed, so doomed beyond knowing.

When I see you again, I would like you to keep the carbon copy of a manuscript (15 stories including the three that you already have) that I am
sending to my agent, in case I lose the original the way I have lost
many valuable manuscripts before. It does not mean that I will ask for
them some day; it only means that I don't want them to be completely lost
to the world.

Take good care of yourself; if something happens to you the world will
not be the same to me. You are all there is in the world, whose
heart truly beats for life, for love even, when the opportune time comes,
which will come to you as to all angels of this sorrowful world.

I will write four more pieces for the JOURNEY AMONG NIGHTINGALES
series, under your name, before I proceed with the following brief
outline of five novels about Pinoys which are interrelated, or inter-
connected, in their various ramifications though they all tend to
encompass Filipino exprience in the United States:

1. A DOOR AGAINST THE SETTING SUN

> A novel based on the life and experience of someone, cover-
> ing the stretch of agricultural territory between El Centro,
> California, and Blaine, Washington, with perhaps a scene or
> two at the salmon canneries in Alaska: Part One, as a worker;
> Part Two, as a labor organizer; Part Three, as a political
> man. Ending upon his arrest as subversive in Seattle, he dies
> in prison, after the "hound" in THE HOUND OF DARKNESS visits
> him. But this last scene, to understand it, takes us to -

2. THE HOUND OF DARKNESS

> The last winter of the "hound's" life, all set with a Seattle
> background, after vindicating all his former friends - long,
> long ago in California including the protagonist in A DOOR
> AGAINST THE SETTING SUN, as indicated in the last scene, which
> is a kind of brief resume of their years of friendship. Vio-
> lently dying at last in the winter of his 35th year, we want
> to know what made him that way, cruel to some and kind to others,
> a dual personality ruthlessly seeking revenge and at the same
> time making amends for grave wrongs that he has committed,
> a haunted, conflicted, venomous mind, but at the same time be-
> wilderingly understanding, quiet, full of pride and honor. So
> we want to know what made him that way, and we find it in -

3. AS LONG AS THE GRASS SHALL GROW

> A novel with a rural California background, perhaps Lompoc,
> covering a winter of 1931, when the "hound" had just arrived
> in America from the Philippines. Here it is presented, in
> part at least, the beginning of the "wound" inflicted upon
> the "hound" which became bigger as time went by, although the
> story itself covers only one winter, upon his escape from the
> lynching party across a snowfilled rugged mountain, leaving
> behind him three dead dear friends . . .

4. WHAT FOOLS WE ARE

> A novel whose materials are taken from a Northwest Pacific
> exprience but transposed to Los Angeles, from the present
> time to the period between THE HOUND OF DARKNESS and ALL THE
> CONSPIRATORS, the last of the five novels in the cicle, it
> deals with a love affair woven around two themes, political
> struggle (on the part of the woman) and financial quandary
> (on the part of the man). There is a great difficulty in
> a story like this, when you want to avoid the stereotype
> kind, because you have to go deep in the hearts of both,
> and their various experiences that shaped their individuali-
> ties. But in -

5. ALL THE CONSPIRATORS (or perhaps it will be THE HOUSE OF ALMANZOR)
> This problem is somewhat revealed and explained, although the
> protagnoist here is one who appeard briefly toward the middle
> of A DOOR AGAINST THE SETTING SUN and again, of course, in
> WHAT FOOLS WE ARE. Actually, it is the story of Pinoy whox
> sacrificed his life and future to raise a family of American
> born children - two sons and a daughter - upon the trick of
> a marriage that tricked him all his life, so that the mother
> is gone when the story opens upon this scene: The two sons are
> grown; the younger finishing college (a communist?), the other
> has a small parish but due for a promotion (a piest), and even-
> tually, whom is the last hope of the father, runs off with
> a Negro. The story here is the betrayal of one brother to the
> FBI, on one hand, and the elopement of the daughter; and put
> together it breaks the father. This concludes a lifetime of
> experience, of a life brimming with tragedies including love
> which is also treated as targedy.

Dear Florentino,

I just came in the office of this union - from jail - and found yout letter. I am happy to know that your wife found enough material in my letter for her thesis. I will answer your letter without a plan; I will put down my ideas as they come to my mind. When a person just came out of jail (drinking?) his mind wanders in a nightmare that pursued him the night before. Now a long time ago I made a resolution never to reveal certain facets of my personal life; I resolved also not to give to anyone a complete bibliography of my published writings. But I will make an exception for your wife's sake, because it is the only way that I can help her. I had a great yearning for formal education, but the time was against me: there were many things against me. There was no one to help me; there was no one to guide me. Then came the awful diseases that wrecked my life forever. (1) If Epifanion Ramos claims something, let him. And I request you to feel not unkindly toward me, because this is <u>one</u> thing that I like to keep for myself. But when I am dead, I really don't care what some people claim;whhose who seem to know me in the long-ago. Of course, I went beyond the primary grades; altogether, however, I spent six years going to school. From this, I hope, your wife can make her own sleuthhhgg This is all I can say about my formal education. (2) My politico-economic ideas are embodied in all my writings but more concrete in poetry. Here let me remind you that THE LAUGHTER OF MY FATHER is not humor; it is satire: it is an indictment against an economic system that stifled the growth of the primitive, making him decadent overnight without passing through the various stages of growth and decay as evidenced by peoples of dead civilizations and those that are dying today. The hidden bitterness in this book is so pronounced in another series of short stories that the Publishers refrained from publishing it for the time being: THE MAN WHO ¶OUND HAPPINES. Even the title is a mockery; he never found happiness. In my first volume of poetry - LETTER FROM AMERICA - are found most of my socio-economic views; but my politico-economic views are found in THE VOICE OF BATAAN; my views on the racial issues in the United States are found in stories I have written for <u>The New Masses</u>, <u>Masses & Mainstream</u>, <u>Common Ground</u>, <u>The New Republic</u>, etc. Read "As Long As The Grass Shall Grow", reprinted in the <u>Philippines Free Press</u>. I used to have pages of political poetry in the Philippine Herald Mid-Week Magazine, when Fred Mangahas was editor. I submitted a large manuscript of poetry to the First Commonwealth Literary Contest; the social upheaval in the thirties was the central theme of all the pieces in this series. I did not win a prize (why should I?), but Nelly X. Burgos, now Mrs. Mangahas, wrote a study of my poetry which was published in the magazine that Fred was then editing. I don't have a copy of the poems, but I believe the title was SHADOW OF THE TERROR. If you ever find a copy of that manuscript... I have given away, and destroyed, hundreds of poems and stories and articles. Unfortunately, I don't have my papers in Seattle, otherwise I would be able to send you some poems relevant to the subject discussed above. There is one woman here who has a collection of my published works; I will try to get in touch with her, and send you some pieces to illustrate my point. Recently (product of the cold war?), I have been writing love poetry and other lyrics. I write everything on the typewriter including poetry. I forgot to mention in my other letter that there is a Persian poet who gas influenced my own poetry - Hassim Kismet.(3) Dates, titles, magazines will follow this letter. (4) I am Cecilio Baroga. I also have a pen name for juvenile books (2 published so far - for the 8-12 age group). (5) I do like to visit the Philippines, but if I do, I doubt if I can come back. All my people are dead; only some young relatives that I have never known personally are left. I have two brothers in the United States, and a niece who, I believe, is taking her PH D or something like that in California. She is the most "educated" person in our whole tribe. My father and mother could not read and write; and two sisters the same; and many, many relatives. I am not an American citizen; I have never applied for it. When you were here I was still unknown; I could not know you then. I have not received <u>Philippine Harvest</u>; I would like to have a copy. I did not know "Freedom From Want" was included in <u>Reading & Writing the Essay</u>: please send me a copy. Now I will try to give you a brief and incomplete bibliography of my writings: THE LAUGHTER OF MY FATHER: Harcourt Brace & Co., New York, 1944; Bantam Books, New York, 1946; Michael & Josephs, London, 1945; Copenhagen, Denmark; Milan, Italy; Jugoslavia; Canada (in French); AMERICA IS IN THE HEART, Harcourt Brace & Co., New York, 1946; Milan, Italy; Canada (in French); THE VOICE OF BATAAN Coward-McCann, New York, 1943; London, 1944; LETTER FROM AMERICA, Decker Press, Illinois, 1942; Chorus For America, Star & Wagon, Los Angeles; The Dark People (10 poems and ten stories), Destinies, California; two juveniles published by Longsman & Green and translated into Swedish and Danish.

A. Uncollected short stories are published in the following magazines: The New Yorker, Town & Country, Harper's Bazaar, Mademoiselle, New Masses, Masses & Main stream, Common Ground, Western Review, Kansas Magazine, University of Kansas City Review, Arizona Quarterly Magazine, Destinies, Script, Interim, and Manila magazines. B. Uncollected articles in the following magazines: The New Republic, The New Masses, Town & Country, Books (University of Oklahoma), Pic, Worker (London), Trabajo (Mexico City). Uncollected poetry in the following magazines: Poetry (Chicago); Voices (New York); Lyric (Virginia); Saturday Review of Literature (New York); London; and Manila publications. NOTE: The uncollected short stories are too numerous to write all the titles. However, I am collecting them now under two titles: A VIRGIN FOR COUSIN PEDRO and other tales of Luzon, THE MAN WHO FOUND HAPPINESS. The uncollected published poems are also too numerous; and there are thousands of unpublished pieces in the safekeeping of friends all over the Pacific Coast. C. I am included in the following anthologies and textbooks: A TREASURY OF AMERICAN LAUGHTER (Simon & Schuster); SPELL OF THE PACIFIC (McMillan); LAW IN ACTION (Crown Publishers); AN AMERICAN TREASURY (American Book Company), a university textbook; BEST AMERICAN SHORT STORIES OF 1945 (Houghton & Mifflin); LIVE UP TO LIFE (2nd high school textbook); Henry Holt & Company; WORLD PROSE & POETRY FOR YOUTH, ENGLISH FOR WORLD YOUTH (these are two are edited by Salvador Lopez for Singer Co. of New Jersey, a textbook publishing company; THE FOUR FREEDOMS (a brochure published by the U S government; plus the Philippine anthologies: PHILIPPINE PROSE & POETRY, IV.; PHILIPPINE CROSS-SECTION; FILIPINO ESSAYS IN ENGLISH; READING AND WRITING THE ESSAY. I have never kept track of my writing. In fact, I don't have a single copy of any of my books or any of the magazines where my works are published. I always consult the local public library. I am included in WHO'S WHO IN AMERICA, WHO'S WHO ON THE PACIFIC COAST, TWENTIETH CENTURY AUTHORS (1855-1955), CURRENT BIOGRAPHY, Volume YI. THE LAUGHTER OF MY FATHER was condensed in World Digest, London; some chapters were published in translation in L'Europeo, Milan; also a Danish magazine. If you ever intent to include any of my writings use "As Long As The Grass Shall Grow", a story; or "I Am Not A Laughing Man", an article (The Writer, Boston); or my latest love lyrics (unpublished). I have a two-page biography in Wilson's Library Bulletin, April 1946. I am not working on volume of two of my autobiography, MY LETTER TO THE WORLD; and the first of five novels centering around the Filipino theme on the Pacific Coast - THE HOUND OF DARKNESS, A DOOR AGAINST THE SETTING SUN, ALL THEY CONSPIRATORS, WHAT FOOLS WE ARE, THE HOUSE AJMANZOR...I hope this is incomplete material is of some use to your wife. Extend my best wishes to Leopoldo Yabes. If you want to know some of my personal habits see the following people: P. C. Morantte (Publicity Director for PAL); Jess Villanor, the wartime hero; Leonides Virata; Fred Mangahas; Fred Castro (of the Malacanang); Senators Salipada Pindatun, Macario Peralta; Amadeo Dacanay; Mrs. Pilar Lim; Zameida Quezon; Salvador Lopez (in France?); Prof. Arnaldo Solomon; Prof. Alfonso Santos (of U.P.); Proceso Sebastian (of Cagayan); Governor Juan Rodriguez (of Pangasinan); and Santos the short story writer. They knew only briefly, except Morantte. Of course, I am sending my best wishes to Maximo Ramos (I was helping a big asparagus strike in Stockton when he was in Frisco) and Jose Hernandez and Locsin of the Free Press. I am really more political than most writers and professors in the Philippines suspect. Before I forget, Yabes mimeographed an article of mine entitled "My Education": you should read his copy; I don't have any. It was to come out here, but the censors stopped it. Yes, now that I remember: this particular piece is good for your future anthologies. Let me hear from you. And send me those books. Always contact me through this union, unless you here that I am in California - and you can use the Hollywood address. That is the house of the famous movie camerman, James Wong Howe, a Chinese who has a brother in our native land. His wife is a writer; she is the the "Alice" in AMERICA IS IN THE HEART; her sister is the Dorothy on the dedicatory page of CHORUS FOR AMERICA AND THE LAUGHTER OF MY FATHER. The officers of this union are attending a union convention in Long Beach, California, this week. Most of the officers are from Narvacan, except the president (San Manuel, Pangasinan) and the vice president (Aringay, La Union). Yabes has an uncle or something here - he was my mentor about twenty years ago - Don Yabes, 229 W. 22nd Street, Tuczon, Arizona. What is Gabriel Manalac doing now? My greetings to him. I was the late Confesor's guide and secretary when he was here for a briefperiod. Perhaps you read somewhere that I was married? Oh, the things they write about me. I have never been married, and perhaps never will get married. I don't know yet what to do. However, I am about to make a decision. I am contemplating to work in the salmon cannries in Alaska this summer; or return to California where I have been offered to edit a magazine. Did you hear I like to drink? If you were here with me now I could show you something for your students. I can down a gallon of wine in one setting; mo t of the officers here are heavy drinkers especially the president and the secr

PARTIAL BIBLIOGRAPHY

BOOKS PUBLISHED:
LETTER FROM AMERICA (Poetry); James Decker Press, Prairie City, Illinois; March, 1952
CHORUS FOR AMERICA (Poetry Anthology); Star & Wagon, Los Angeles; March, 1942.
THE DARK PEOPLE (Ld poems, 50 stories); Destinies Press, Mountain View, Calif.; Sept.1943
THE VOICE OF BATAAN (narrative poetry); Coward-McCann, New York; Spring 1943
   "     "     "     "     same          Hogarth Press, London;  Autumn 1944
   "     "     "     "     a portion included in PROSE & POETRY OF THE WORLD; L. W. Singer & Co.;
                                           Newark, New Jersey; 1954
   "     "     "     "     a portion included in ENGLISH FOR WORLD YOUTH, 3rd & 4th Year;
                                           American Book Company, New York; 1954
THE LAUGHTER OF MY FATHER (stories); Harcourt, Brace & Company; New York; April 1944
   "     "     "     "     reprinted by Bantam Books, New York; summer 1946.
   "     "     "     "     published in England by Michael Josephs; Fall 1945
   "     "     "     "     translated into Danish; Caspar Nielson Compnay, Copenhagen, 1945
   "     "     "     "     translated into Italian for Enaudi Company; Milan, Italy; 1945
   "     "     "     "     translated into Swedish; 1946
   "     "     "     "     translated into French (Canada) 1953
   "     "     "     "     translated into Joguslavian; Belgrade 1953
AMERICA IS IN THE HEART (autobiography); Harcourt, Brace & Company; New York; 1946
   "     "     "     "     translated into Italian for Enaudi Company; Milan, Italy; 1947
A Juvenile on the Igorots (under a pen name); Longmann, Green & Company; New York;1944
   "     "     "     "     translated into Swedish; 1946
A Juvenile on the Moros (under same pen name); Longmans, Green & Company; New York; 1946
   "     "     "     "     translated into Swedish 1948
Uncollected stories published in the following magazines (dates missing) - The New Yorker,
   Town & Country, Harper's Bazaar, Mademoiselle, New Masses, Masses & Mainstream,
   Common Ground, Western Review, Kansas Magazine, University of Kansas City Review,
   Arizona Quarterly Review, Destinies, Sxcript, Interim, and Manila publications :
   1) The Bandit and the Tax Collector, 2) The Great Lover,91 Would Be Living,
   4) As Long As The Grass Shall Grow, 5) The Farmer and the Priest, 6) My Village was Enchanted, 7) The Will of my Father, 8) The Summertime of my Father,
   9)The Springtime of my Father,10) My Father was a Soldier, 11) The Courtship
   of Uncle Ponso, 12) A Beggar Came to Town, 13) The Lonesome Soldier, 14) The
   Story of a Letter, 15) A Virgin forx Cousin Pedro, 16) Store on the Highway,
   17) A Trip with Father, 18) My Brother's Short Stay, 19) The Little Faith,
   20) The Amorous Ghost, 21) My Cousin's Vicente's Homecoming, 22) My Brother
   Osong's career in Politics, 23) The Champion Hag-Stealer, 24) A Rich Man
   in the Family, 25) The Power of Music, 26) The Silence,27)The End of the War
Uncollected articles published in the following magazines (dates and some titles missing) -
   The New Masses, The New Republic, Books, The Writer, Town & Country, Pic,
   Worker (London), Tabajo (Mexico City): The Cultural Heritage of the Filipino
   People, Rizal and the Philippine Tradition, Freedom From Want, Letter To
   America, The Death of Otis Ferguson, My First Day in America, Writing in the
   Philippines Today, I Am Not A Laughing Man, Letter to a Filipino & Woman
   (Mrs. Salvador Lopez), etc.
Numerous uncollected poems imcluding the following:"Bataan", (Saturday Review of Literature,
   New York; March 20, 1043; "Letter In Exile","Sunset And Evening Star", American
   History (Poetry, Chicago), April 1942; "Without Ceremony", Letter From America",
   "In Time of Drought","No Story", "Monuments" (Poetry, Chicago), Feb.1941;
   "These Are Also Living" (Poetry, Chicago) Aug 1938; dozens in Voices, New York;
   Script, Beverly Hills; Lyric, Virginia, Westward, San Francisco; Contemporary
   Verse, New York; Westminster Magazine, Oglethorpe University; "Interlude:
   Song of the War", Saturday Review of Literature, Feb. 12, 1944; "Now You Are
   Still", Saturday Review of Literature, October 14, 1944.
ANTHOLOGIES  where my writings are included: SCHOLASTIC ANTHOLOGY 1947; A TREASURY OF
   AMERICAN LAUGHTER (Simon & Schuster); SMELL OF THE PACIFIC (MCMillan); LAW IN
   ACTION (Crown Publishers); AN AMERICAN TREASURY (American Book Company);
   BEST AMERICAN SHORT STORIES OF 1945 (Houghton & Mifflin Co); LIVE UP TO LIFE
   (Henry Holt & Co.); PHILIPPINE CROSS-SECTION (Manila), PHILIPPINE PROSE &
   POETRY, VOL. 1V0Manila), FILIPINO ESSAYS IN ENGLISH (Manila); READING AND
   WRITING THE ESSAY (Manila); PROSE & POETRY OF THE WORLD (New York, L. W.
   Singer & Co.); ENGLISH FOR WORLD YOUTH (American Book Co., New York).
FIRST DRAFTS OF - THE CRY AND THE DEDICATION, an 800-page novel based on the Huks move-
   ment; 30 retold Philippine Folk tales; ±9xxkxxkxxxkxxkxxkxxkxxfxxyxxagxxkx
   3 one-act plays; 57 short stories; over 300 poems; a few articles
UNPUBLISHED (as of this date): A book of Verse for Children; THE TALL GRAY HORSE &
   THE ROOSTER'S EGG (two juveniles); NOW YOU ARE STILL (a collection of


And published poems); 29 new short stories in the hands of my agent
   works in progress. Sorry can't give all exact dates

[June 12, 1953]
Saturday

Dear Mary,

Thanks for the reading material, the basket of fruits and candies, the rose tree and the reading matter. Thanks also for the delightful visit.

When you came that first time but could not pass through the gate, I wrote you a letter thanking you for the gifts. I often wondered if that letter reached you; I used an address I found in one of the books. In this connection, I gave your books to Marion K.; I hope she returned them to you. Thanks, too, for these first gifts.

I did not realize that you are younger than what I had imagined. When I first met you some years ago, I had a few drinks and naturally my eyes were poor. Besides, I remember that the house had a very poor lighting system. And when I met you again at Irene's house, I was fifteen feet away from you. We did not even talk to each other. Perhaps you noticed last night that I tried to be as close to you as possible; I am nearsighted, and my hearing has been greatly affected by the medications I have been taking here.

But I did appreciate your conviviality and openness. There are many poor conversationalists, and they sometimes make me want to run away. I want you to talk always freely the way you did last night. We can learn from each other that way. And when I see you again, I'd like you to tell me about yourself. Or we could talk about books and writing. Or you could ask me questions. Would you like that?

I forgot to mention that I may go out of this soon — perhaps sometime in July. So I would like to see more of you, and to know you better. I like you to be my friend always.

This is my permanent address as long as I am in the USA: 1562 Queens Road, Hollywood, Calif. But you can always reach me through my publishers.

I am giving you these addresses because I don't know how long I will be in Seattle. My stay in your city depends on a few vital factors.

I may have a Town leave in a few weeks. And if I do, I would like to invite you for dinner. Of course, I will drop you a note.

I am enclosing a poem written this morning. This part is published in Saturday Review under the same title. I always write in series, because each work inspires the next. I hope you will enjoy the poem.

The man with you — I did not catch his name?

Now, don't hesitate to know me. I am just a peasant who became literate, and full of love for everyone —

Carlos Bulosan

"You are a good bitch," he said, stimulated now ~~with~~ by the bedroom conversation that he had known in that other land, after loving. unaffected

"Were they big?"

"What are you talking about?"

"The American women you have known." She made an obscene gesture with ~~Max~~ her hands.

He looked at her ~~with~~ astonishment. Curiosity? No. Blind jealousy? No. Perhaps both. Yes, that was it. Both.

So he said, "I don't know what you mean."

She knew he did not want to talk about it. She might drive him away from her, and she did not want to do that now that it had been done. She did not want to lose him now that she had ~~gax~~ given herself to him. That she could not do now ~~that~~ because she felt close to him, closer than she had ever been to anyone including Fedilio of long ago. And instinctively she felt he was her man now. ~~And~~ ~~~~ She knew now ~~that~~ she could not give herself wholly to anyone. That Mabini affair was her duty....

"Kiss me," she said.

He kissed her.

"Tell me you love me."

"I love you."

She put his hand on her hot breasts. "Come," she said.

He lay ~~down~~ beside her. They talked for some time. Then sleep came, as sleep always comes after loving. a satisfactory It was a dreamless and untroubled sleep. Two yellow butterflies sprang from somewhere and hovered about them, flitting from grass to grass, and mated. Then they winged their way to the trees.

They sleep ~~for~~ an hour. When Dante opened his eyes, Dabu was standing beside them. He ~~was~~ awakened Mameng.

"Well?" Dabu greeted them.

Dante rose and helped Mameng to her feet. They looked at each other with secret understanding. They brushed off the fringes of dead grass on their clothes.

- "We, ~~have~~ fallen asleep," Dante said.

"I thought you had been lost," Dabu said.

"What is up?"

"What is up? You would have been shot dead for all I know. Who will take care of Mameng if you are not careful? And you asked me what is up!"

"I knew you would be watching out for us."

Dabu poked Dante with a finger between the ribs. "Is everything all right?" he asked.

Dante did not answer him. Mameng looked searchingly in Dabu's glittering small eyes, and she knew that he knew. She did not say anything. She busied herself with her knapsack.

"You must have forgotten the passage of time," Dabu said.

"We surely have," Dante said.

"We have been waiting for you. Lunch was ready an hour ago."

Dante slapped him on the back. "Is that right?" he said.

Dabu laughed and repeated, "Is that right?" Then he said in a low tone of voice, "The old man is drunk as hell."

"It is bad."

"I know that old man. There is nothing to worry about."

"Is this not his ~~territory~~ territory?"

"It is."

"Then that is the reason for it. Memories."

"He will sleep it off. He and Hassim will go down to the plain after lunch."

"Are you sure?"

"I think they will."

"But why?"

"It is a part of our mission."

Dante looked at Dabu. ~~longingly.~~ Then he said, "Yes, I understand now. Legaspi will ~~nextxxxxx~~ be next, then you...,"

Dabu's laughing face changed. "You should watch out for yourself," he said. ~~XXX~~ "Eh, Mameng?"

Mameng punched _him_ lightly ~~,~~ on the stomach. "Enough of that now."

Dabu's face changed again. He laughed and took their arms. They started climbing up the hill through the tall grass. There was no breeze now and their shirts were soaked through with perspiration. Dante wanted to look back to where they had lain, but Dabu was holding _them_ tightly. Dabu was climbing up the hill with his head down, as though he were carrying a heavy load on his back. As they climbed up the hill with him, they both knew ~~that~~ they were leaving a memory whose true nature was finally resolved; and having resolved it, they knew ~~that~~ they had done a duty to themselves and to the others. So they silently climbed up the hill with Dabu, and when they reached the crown Dante stopped and looked back. Dabu and Mameng looked back, too. They stood side by side looking down the hillside, thinking of what had been done. _And_ They knew without saying it that something important had ~~is~~ just been accomplished, which had _finally_ resolved itself into its true dignity. Then they turned around and walked to the others, thinking now that all of it was the ~~same~~ _total_ vanquishment of the shame.

\*\*\*\*

Dunstan Peyton
P.O. Box 6055
Petrol Station
Los Angeles 55, Calif.

Canned for 3ᵈ ʲᵘˢ⁾ ᵖ⁻ⁱᵃⁱ

## The MY FILIPINO HOUSEBOY

Dunstan Peyton

The other day, When I was rummaging in his favorite bookshop, he found a book written by his former Filipino houseboy. He was somewhat amused because when the houseboy left me fifteen years before he had said something about going into the writing business. He had not given it a thought at the time. But as he opened the book, he was thrilled with envy. Now I discovered that the houseboy had written several books, and two of them had been reviewed favorably by critics and made considerable sales. He bought them all and went home, remembering back to the years when Conrado Bustamante was in his employ.

Dunstan Peyton had written a novel in 1936 which was bought by one of the Hollywood movie studios for what he then considered a great sum of money. It is a common practice in the movie industry to sign up a writer whose book or story is purchased for picturization. And that was how he went to Hollywood, lucky enough to have a five-year contract, lucky enough to escape from his small dark room in Brooklyn. As soon as he had settled myself in a house, he was advised by his new friends to have a Filipino houseboy. These friends had Filipino houseboy themselves, so they were in the position to appraise the qualities and virtues of houseboys. He understood from them that Filipino houseboys were neat, efficient, courteous and inexpensive. Well, he consented.

Conrado went to my house through the amazing chain of circumstances that is common among houseboys in Hollywood and Beverly Hills. One of his friends told his Filipino houseboy about his need, so the houseboy passed it on to his friends; and the next morning, before he had my coffee, Conrado appeared at the door.

He had expected an older man, but he was confronted by a Filipino who was probably nineteen. And of course he was small and frail, but he had a pleasant smile through which peeped out well-formed clean teeth. His